RAINSWEPT

and other stories

R O N S C O T T

ISBN: 978-1-5356-1264-7

Dedicated to Steve,

who is my hero

Preface

Someone once said that all fiction is autobiographical. Perhaps, but the connections to the author's life will often be buried in several layers of his or her unconscious. Perhaps it is more realistic to suspect that all fiction is, in some way, biographical to the reader. When a reader finds a way to relate, or identify, with a piece of fiction, the reader is making that made-up story become personal.

Someone else, however, observed that all fiction is truth, and here we are on firmer ground. Story, to have meaning, must be about truth. We will have little interest in wasting time reading stories in which we cannot find truth.

Hopefully, the stories in *Rainswept and Other Stories* fall into this category. Part one, "Truth in Story," includes three seemingly dissimilar fictional tales linked in that they arise from three aspects of my life experiences. They each are fiction, but they each are drawn from – and address – a real world.

Part two, "True Stories," are non-fiction, and therefore intentionally attempt to tell true stories. Two are memoir, while the third, "Making Something Happen: The Hugs and Kisses Project," tells an inspiring story arising from the 9 – 11 tragedies.

Part three, "Fables and Fantasy," again tells three stories, a bit further removed from reality. Only one of these stories, Reverie," is a memoir of sorts. Finally, a few short personal essays complete the collection.

One cannot write and collect such stories without help. I should especially mention my wife and partner of more than 45 years, Marilyn Scott. She has read everything I have written, and if she does not like something, I listen. Again, as with the first collection, *Reflections from Miri's Woods*, Will Ridley and Barbara Levin have provided encouragement and occasional nudges.

Ron Scott

Kirkwood, MO

December 2018

Contents

RAINSWEPT

and other stories

Truth in Story

Rainswept

The old woman glanced out the kitchen window, looking at the driving rain. She pulled on her boots, the red ones that came almost to her knees, and put on the yellow rain slicker and the green cap with "Grandma" on it.

She looked at the kitchen clock. Almost 9:00 AM. The post office would be opening; she needed to leave. She frowned, pursing her lips; then, reaching for an umbrella, went through the door. On the steps she pulled the door shut behind her, locking it. She frowned again, and reached into the pocket of the slicker. Finding the small purse and key, she opened the umbrella and started down the steps.

The wind hit her immediately, throwing her off balance. She caught herself and moved down the walk toward the road. Turning left, she leaned into the wind and began to walk, watching the ground before each step. As had become her custom in recent weeks she counted each step.

This was a familiar two blocks: she walked to the post office every day except Sunday at this time. And most days she made additional trips the same way, to the IGA, a block beyond, or the bank, a block the other way. So, she walked without thinking, counting, two blocks and then turning left, without looking around, fighting the wind in her umbrella.

She was surprised when she realized that she was lost. It made no sense. She knew the way, made this trip every day. Had they changed the roads overnight? Disoriented, fighting panic, unsure what to do, she kept walking, looking for something familiar, anything that could tell her where she was.

When the farmer, driving through the storm, passed the old woman walking down the highway she was three-quarters of a mile from town. Buffeted by the wind, she had lost her umbrella. Squinting through his wiper-streaked windshield he thought he recognized her, slowed, then stopped and backed up.

"Mrs. Stewart, is that you? What are you doing out here? It's raining pitchforks! Let me give you a ride."

She peered at him without recognition, frowned, and shook her head. It was not safe to get into a strange man's car. Just a little farther and she would find Main Street and the Post Office. She continued to walk down the highway. The man hesitated, shook his head, and drove on into town.

When he got to the IGA he parked, went in, and borrowed a phone to call the Sheriff. Twenty minutes later, when the deputy found the old woman, she was stumbling along the road, crying.

"There you are, Mrs. Stewart! Are you lost?" He got out of the car, took her by the hand, and helped her into the patrol car. "Where in the world were you going, Mrs. Stewart?" Shivering, her sobbing subsiding, she looked at him without reply.

"What are we going to do with you, Mrs. Stewart?" he said, shaking his head.

After a few minutes, however, the old woman seemed to pull herself together. "That's a good one on me!" she laughed. "I don't know how I could have become lost on a two-block walk I take every day. It must have been the rain."

Relieved, the deputy decided to take her home.

"Could you stop at the Post Office?" she asked. "I have to get my mail."

When the man's wife came home he was piling clothes on the bed, packing for a trip of indeterminate length. She could see that he was upset as she began to put her own clothes on the bed as well. He looked at her, frowning.

"I'm going with you. You're going to need all the support you can get." Then, after a pause, "Did you call her? How is she?"

Feelings of relief cascaded into the anger he had been fighting. He grunted, went into the bathroom and began to stuff toiletries into a travel case.

"Yeah. I don't know. Can you get off?"

"I told them it was a family emergency. It is, isn't it?"

"I guess."

He walked into the closet and stood fingering his clothes, fighting tears. He did not want her to see him crying. Taking a deep breath, he walked back into the room.

"Thanks," he mumbled, hurrying out of the room.

≈

The old woman watched through the window as the man in the uniform walked back to his car, got in, and drove away. She frowned, pursing her lips. Then she pulled her slicker back on, put on her cap, and went back out into the rain, which had settled into a steady drizzle.

She walked across the street, entered the front door of the green house on the corner, and called, "Marie?"

Marie was in the kitchen, as usual, baking pies for Crumbles, the only restaurant in town. She had glanced out the window as the patrol car drove up, had seen the old woman get out.

"You'll never believe what happened!" The old woman laughed, a strange, forced laugh. Beginning with her preparations for the trip to the post office she zigzagged through the story. "I can't believe I got lost on a trip I take every day!" Another laugh.

"Ruth, what in the world were you doing going out into that rain just to go to the Post Office? Your mail's not that important and it would be open all day anyway!" Marie's scolding tone grated, wounding the old woman.

"Well, it was all right. I had my boots on." She pointed down to her legs. "They come almost to my knees. And this raincoat. And my umbrella." Frowning, she laughed again. "Although that umbrella was no use at all. The wind just turned it inside out. And when I pulled it down again the wind snatched it away! I was better off without it!"

"What are we going to do with you, Ruth?" Marie continued, scolding. "Sometimes you just don't think right!"

"Well," said the old woman, "I just came over to tell you that you didn't have any mail." Pursing her lips again, feeling anger she could not acknowledge, the old woman went back out into the rain and returned to her own house.

〰〰

Later, driving, the man and his wife talked a little.

"What did she say when you called her?"

He was silent a moment, organizing his thoughts. "Well, at least she admitted getting lost." A pause. "At first, she said it was really raining hard, but when I jumped her about going out in it she backed off." He paused again, then, sarcastically, "Said it wasn't that bad. She had her boots on — 'that come almost to my knees' — and a raincoat and 'I wasn't getting all that wet.' Another pause. " And she had to get the mail."

"Did you tell her we were coming?"

"I told her I was coming — I didn't know if you could go." A pause. "She said I didn't need to — she was fine. I said I was coming anyway."

"Who called you?"

"Sheriff's Deputy. Picked her up on the highway a mile south of town." A pause. "And JoAnn from the IGA. And Marie." Another pause. "And Bob Martin."

"Who's Bob Martin?"

"The new Pastor, I think. He said half the town called him."

"One thing about a small town — everybody knows what's going on with everybody else."

The man grunted, fell silent again.

"Well, one thing's for certain," she said. "This time we have to do something. We have to force her to make a choice." She paused to assess the silence. "Either come back with us or go into a home there."

His jaw tightened again. At first, he said nothing, uncomfortable with his anger. Finally, shrugging his shoulders, he said, "I don't know. When your mother doesn't know enough to come in out of the rain, what are you going to do?"

〰〰

The old woman looked at the kitchen clock. Almost eleven; past time for dinner. She was exhausted, felt frightened, but she had to keep moving. She went to the refrigerator, pulled out a foil-wrapped sweet potato, unwrapped one end, and began to nibble on it. Taking a frozen package from the freezer she put it in a bowl, put the bowl in the microwave, and set the dial on 1,000.

What was it Donny said — it's not really 1,000 seconds? She could never grasp his insisting that the dial referred to minutes, not seconds. That made no sense to her. So, she just kept doing it the way she always had, the way that worked for her.

She walked into the living room, pacing. The old cat raised her head, meowed, and arched her back as the woman petted her.

5

"Did you miss me, Isabella? Don't be angry! I just got lost." She rambled on, a fragmented stream-of-consciousness: "I hope Donny doesn't find out — he'll be furious! Have you eaten? Yes, a little; good! Boy, I was scared, 'Bella. It was really raining! Reminds me of the time I was caught in the rain back on the farm, walking back from — I don't remember whose place I was visiting. I got soaked! Dad was really furious! He had gone looking for me, but he went down the wrong road. How 'bout a little more food? Oh — my dinner is probably ready."

Returning to the kitchen she removed the barely thawed vegetable packet from the microwave. Pressing it out of the zip-lock bag into the bowl, she placed it on the table, turned on the TV, sat down, and began to absently push cold vegetables into her mouth.

Beginning to cry, she shook her head, frowned, and pursed her lips. She fought back tears as she continued to eat.

♒

Silence descended on Don and his wife as they drove. Unsure what to say, she closed her eyes and drifted toward sleep. Don was lost in reverie, driving by instinct. His mind wandered through subjects, some relevant, some avoidant. Fighting tears, he felt waves of anger interspersed with fear, streaked with growing sadness.

He had always had a difficult time with his mother. No, that's not quite right: he had always had a hard time going home, but until recently didn't realize that it was with her. Most of his life he had assumed that his problem was with his father — adopted father, really, but he had always minimized the relationship.

Bennett Stewart had been a hard man, angry, violence always evident just beneath the surface. He was easy to blame, a willing scapegoat, and Don had always been afraid of him.

But that was the way she wanted it, Don thought. Only in the last few years had he come to understand the covert alliance between them when he was a child: how much they each needed to be afraid of Bennett. Donny and his mother had clung to each other in helpless mutual protection, in what had produced, for Don, a constant feeling of impossible obligation. As he came to understand this his anger shifted, away from Bennett — who he began to see as a man of wit and grace trapped in a frustrating life — toward his mother, who he was coming to see as shallow, narcissistic, and of limited capacity.

But it was not an easy transition and, in the years since Bennett had died, it brought new and profound guilt. And a new reservoir of anger, which he had been trying to work through in weekly calls and, in recent years, in visits every two or three months.

Bennett had died – how many years ago? – of cancer, a slow, painful death, made worse by his wife's obsessive nursing. Don had concluded that Bennett "died with more grace than he ever lived with."

Bennett had loved to be outdoors, probably because it got him away from his wife, and he had always fished and hunted. In his declining years he fished almost daily, never really caring whether he caught anything.

The symbols of his interests had always been part of the home's decor: a rod and reel standing in the corner, an old rifle, shotgun, and handgun in a glass-front gun cabinet. After Bennett's death his wife had removed them all, throwing the handgun into a box she shoved into a closet, asking Don to dispose of the rifle and shotgun. Because he disliked guns as much as she did, he gave them to a friend.

Don thought that his mother did fairly well for the first few years after Bennett's death. She had her eccentricities, certainly: for a few years she fed all the town's stray cats; she swore by a strange, restricted diet consisting mainly of boiled vegetables, oatmeal and bananas; and she followed an increasingly regimented pattern of daily activities.

But she had friends, including some shut-ins she visited almost daily, perhaps driving them to distraction with her constant chatter and repetitious storytelling. Don always said that she had only "seventeen stories," so she repeated herself a lot; and she could (and would) convert any subject to herself with one of these stories.

She became known as the "sweater lady" because she compulsively knitted for everyone she knew. She would never accept any payment, and only occasionally noted that she seldom saw anyone wearing one. Don considered them almost unwearable: they were out of style, impossibly heavy, and either too hot or not warm enough; but his mother insisted that the recipients were always very excited to get them.

Don gradually came to understand that the real value of these gifts was what the knitting did for his mother. Always anxious, she had to be doing something "useful." The knitting kept her mind focused, her fingers busy. In fact, in recent months, he noted, she had knitted less, finally stopping, testimony to her deteriorating condition.

With the deterioration came even greater isolation. It was the isolation that frightened Don the most. She – they – had always been isolated, out on that farm. Bennett came and went, but his mother seldom went anywhere. If it had not been for school, Don knew, he would be trapped there too, alone on the farm.

Don had always assumed his mother remained isolated on the farm (and later in the small town to which they moved so Bennett could fish more easily) because Bennett demanded it. But in recent years he had begun to rethink that idea also, recognizing that she kept to herself because she needed it, because she felt safer alone.

He had finally come to understand how frightened his mother had always been. The irony, he saw, was that it was Bennett, who always frightened her most, who provided her security. With Bennett around, she felt protected from outside threats, felt safe. When he was gone the threats gradually closed in.

Bennett had frightened him, too, as a child. But it was the isolation that always overwhelmed Don, terrifying him. Even now, each time he drove home – especially tonight – the oppressiveness grew with each mile.

The silence continued until the pair reached the motel, about half-way to their destination, where they usually spent the night. They registered, carried their gear into the room, and prepared for bed without comment.

∿

The old woman fell asleep watching TV early in the evening, and awoke about 2:30 in the morning. She awoke, apparently from a dream, feeling anxious. Unsure what time it was, she began her morning routine, feeding the cat, cleaning the litter box, taking a sponge bath, getting dressed, and getting her breakfast (oatmeal and a banana).

Something was supposed to happen today, something frightening, but she couldn't remember what it was. And she felt so tired. Every bone ached.

She went into the north bedroom, Bennett's old room. She always felt safer there, somehow. The old cat came in, began nosing into the walk-in closet. When she did not come out the woman followed her into the closet.

"Where are you, 'Bella? Come on out. You'll get dirty in there." The cat was rubbing against a shoe box, and had dislodged the lid.

"What's that? Oh — you found Dad's old gun! Come on, get away from there. You'll hurt yourself!" She poked into the box herself, pushing signs out of the way. "Ugh! I never liked that thing! I'll have to ask Donny to take it away."

She paused for a moment, making mental connections. "That's right! Donny's coming today!" She thought for another moment, then gingerly lifted the handgun out of the box. Carrying it with her left hand she lifted the cat with the other, backing out of the closet. "Let's put this in the kitchen, so we remember to say something to him. Now, come on, let's get you something to eat. You must be starved."

Later, in the kitchen, thinking about Donny coming, she felt a wave of fear. Was he going to try to take her away, make her go home with him?

He had tried once before, years ago. He had tried to make her move with him to the city, but she had refused. She had told him, "No sir! You're not moving me to that city where you live! This is my life!" That had certainly backed him down.

She continued to putter about until almost 8:30. Then, realizing it was about time for the post office to open, she began to get ready to go out.

〰〰

They had fallen to sleep as soon as they got to the motel, but Don slept fitfully, awakening frequently. Each time he awakened he would get up to go to the bathroom, a testament to his aging, but he realized that the culprit was probably the coffee he had drunk the night before to stay awake while he drove.

Finally, about 4:30, as he was replaying the events of the day before, he realized that he was not going to be able to get back to sleep. Still, comforted by his wife's steady breathing, he remained in bed.

Had they finally reached the end of the road? He had decided years ago to let his mother remain on her own if she could take care of herself, as long as it was safe. He had always assumed that moving her, putting her in a home, would probably kill her anyway. But he had also assumed that the end would come when she could not get around, was hurt or too sick to do the things she needed to do.

This "creeping dementia" was, ironically, unexpected. He had noticed her increasing forgetfulness, of course, during his weekly telephone visits; but he attributed that to the forgetfulness of normal aging. It was only recently that he began to realize that there was more to it, that she was having trouble actually making sense out of ordinary things.

Like the microwave: she couldn't understand how the timer worked. The first time she told Don that she set the microwave at "1,000 seconds" to cook a potato he tried to explain: "Mom, that's not 1,000 seconds. That's ten minutes. 1,000 seconds would be (a pause to work the calculator) almost seventeen minutes." But she just couldn't get it, always ending his "explanations" with, "Well, I don't care. I just cook it until it's done." But he was sure that was not the case.

Or her PaceCare service. She had tested her pacemaker by telephone on the third Thursday of each month for years; but recently she has had difficulty determining which Thursday was the third Thursday. Each Thursday she prepared, waiting by the telephone, and then, frustrated, finally called PaceCare. When they would tell her she had the wrong Thursday she would become angry. "It doesn't make any sense, Donny. If they don't want to test me why don't they just say so?"

And now this. Those other things were frustrating, worrisome, but they didn't seem dangerous. But going out in a thunderstorm, getting lost and wandering a mile down the highway — that was dangerous.

When he had called her, yesterday afternoon, after he learned of her getting lost, he tried to tell her how frightened he was for her welfare. As usual, she discounted his fears: she was all right and, besides, he didn't have to worry about her. "You don't need to come. I'm all right."

"Yes, but you could have been seriously hurt. You could have died out there."

"Oh, I don't think so, Donny. It was just a little rain."

"It was a downpour, Mother! It was a fucking flood!"

"You don't have to use that language, Don. If I want to go out in the rain I will. Besides, I had to go to the post office."

"No, you didn't, Mother. You do not get anything that important. Besides, it wouldn't rain that hard for long."

"Well, I don't know. I don't want to talk about it, Donny. I don't want to get all upset." She began to cry.

Donny had picked up a paperweight, fingered it a moment, and then put it down. Reaching over he lifted a small pillow off the couch and, furiously, helplessly, he hurled it against the wall.

"I am coming, Mom. We have to talk about this."

"No, we don't. I'm fine. You don't have to worry about me"

"Oh, Mom. What am I going to do with you?"

It was somewhere in the middle of this reverie that it dawned on him. Of course, he thought: *I have become Bennett.* She needs me to be just as mean as she thought he was. She's afraid of me, just as she was afraid of him.

The force of the realization took his breath away, filled him with mixtures of relief, because so many things now made sense, sadness, that he must play a role he did not want, and anger. He got out of bed, went into the bathroom, sat on the toilet. Realizing that he was crying he turned on the fan to drown the sound of any sobs.

After a while, after he calmed down, he crawled back into bed. It was almost five, and he was exhausted. Diane stirred, turning away from him. Carefully he moved over, curled against her, and reached an arm over her. Comforted, he fell asleep.

They awoke about 6:30, each gradually becoming aware that they were next to the other. He pressed against her, wanting, needing to be held. Diane turned, reached for his hand, and squeezed it. Then, understanding, she helped him remove his briefs, slipped off her own underwear, and pulled him toward her.

They moved together, quietly, without passion, for several minutes. Finally, he stopped, rested his head against hers for a moment, then withdrew and rolled away. Silently he reached and held her hand.

Neither said anything for several minutes. Then she said, "Is there something I can do for you?"

A long silence. Then, "No, it's OK. I should have known better. There's too much going on – too much inside." A pause. "Too many people in the bed. And I guess I'm too tired." Another pause. "I think what I really wanted was to be held." He got out of bed, fleeing again to the bathroom.

"Maybe tonight we can have the bed to ourselves," she said, softly, to his departing backside.

〜〜〜

The old woman went out, on schedule, arriving at the post office just as it opened. She had no mail, but she asked for and got Marie's mail, and started home, counting each step. As she passed Marie's house she turned in, walked in her unlocked door, and laid the two envelopes on the table.

"Marie, here's your mail." Hearing no response, she went back out, crossed the street and went into her own house.

Marie watched through her kitchen window. Since she did not know what to do, and did not want a repeat of yesterday's confrontation, she had said nothing.

Ten minutes later the old woman was out again, walking to the IGA. She ached all over and, forgetting the bottles of Tylenol she had purchased just last week, wanted to buy more.

Returning home, she left again, returning to the IGA, and bought twelve cans of cat food. This time JoAnn Barnard, the manager, was at the register.

"How are you feeling, Mrs. Stewart? You had quite an adventure yesterday."

How did she know? "I'm OK, just a little tired. I can't believe I got lost going to the post office!" Laughter, too exuberant, forced.

"Well, you need to be careful. Is your son coming in today?'

"I don't know." Lips pursed, a frown. "Well, I think maybe he is. Did I tell you that yesterday?"

Realizing she had said too much JoAnn turned away, waiting on the next customer. The old woman reached for her cat food, went out, and began counting the steps home. She continued to frown.

〜〜〜

Don and Diane walked across the road to the Waffle House for breakfast. Both avoided talking, reading sections of the newspaper Don had bought from the box in front of the motel. After breakfast, as they started driving, Don finally spoke about it.

"Well, here's what I think we should do: I think we should give her a choice."

Diane looked dubious. "What choice?"

14

"Well, she can check into the hospital for an evaluation – to see if this – whatever it is – is reversible, or if there's some drug that might help; or she can come back home with us; or she can move into that home – assistant living, or whatever it is."

"Assisted living." A pause. "But how will you get her to agree?"

"I don't think I can. She doesn't have a choice."

"So, you're giving her a choice, but she's really got no choice?"

"Doing nothing, staying there by herself, that's not one of the choices."

"Don, you know you couldn't handle her living with us. Neither of us could. And besides, we're not home all day – we can't watch her, keep her out of trouble."

"Yeah, I know. I don't think she'd go with us anyway. And if she does, we'll have to get her into some place near us."

"Well, you'd better make that clear to her."

"Jesus, Di, nothing's clear to her. That's the problem!"

They fell silent, both stunned by the ferocity of his words. In his mind Don said, "Why dump on her? She's only trying to help." But, aloud, all he could do was mumble, "I'm sorry. That was uncalled for."

Diane also said nothing, turning instead to look out the window.

A few miles later she turned back. "Do you think we could find someone to move in with her, to live there? Not to 'take care of her' – she'd never accept that – just to 'share expenses.' It is a big house, after all, with a lot of empty space." A pause. And she could watch things for us."

Don's thoughts poised on the verge of listing all the reasons why that idea could never work. He even said, "Well, I don't know. . . ." But then he fell silent, wondering if it might not work after all.

♒

15

The old woman sat on the chair by the window, holding the cat in her lap. "They'll be here soon, 'Bella. You'll see!" She chattered on, wandering through subjects, bouncing off memory, current time, and future fears, while the old cat purred contentedly.

"You know how it is, don't you, 'Bella? It's not easy to live alone. I don't always handle things right. Maybe I'd feel safer with Donny. Like it was with Dad – Sometimes he was mean, sometimes I was afraid of him but usually I felt safer." She paused to look out the window again. "But I don't want to go to the big city! What do you think, 'Bella? What should we do?"

The old cat, almost totally deaf, just purred.

〰〰

Don and Diane pulled into town about 10:30, driving down Main Street to the four-way stop. But instead of turning left for the two blocks to the house Don drove on, pulling in to the IGA parking lot.

Inside the store he asked for JoAnn Barnard. She waved from the back of the store. "I'm sure glad to see you two!"

"How bad was it, JoAnn?"

"It was a real bad rain – wind and hail, really bad. I understand she was way out on Route 43. She must have turned one time too many." JoAnn busied herself sorting produce. "What are you going to do?"

"I don't know," Don said. One minute I want to move her to a home, and the next I hope I can find a way to let her stay there."

"We were wondering if there might be someone that could live with her, maybe – help keep her out of trouble," said Diane. "It's a pretty big house."

JoAnn looked up, surprised. "You know, Dorothy Andrews might be interested. She told me the other day she was going to have to move. She's pretty sharp, but she's in a wheelchair, and she doesn't

16

have much money." A thoughtful pause. "Could your Mom's place be fixed up, so she could get in and out?"

"Sure, I suppose. Shouldn't be that hard to put in a ramp or two."

"Tell you what – I'll see Mrs. Andrew later today, when I deliver her groceries. I'll see if she might be interested."

〜〜〜

The old woman watched the car pull into the drive. She had become more agitated as the morning progressed, and as she became more distressed she became more confused. She wanted to please Donny, wanted him to make her safe. Of course, she would do what he said. But she didn't want to move. This was her home. She could be OK here, couldn't she?

She went to the door, stopped, and went back to the table to pick up Bennett's old pistol. She wanted to show it to Don, to get him to take the gun away.

"Well," said Don, pulling into the drive, "here goes nothing." He cut the engine, sat in the car for a minute, and then unbuckled his seatbelt. Diane waited for him to move first. He had seen his mother looking out of the back porch window, and wondered briefly why she took so long to come out. He shut the car door and started toward the house.

When she did come out she seemed older, somehow, even more frail than usual. She held on to the wooden railing with one hand, the other hanging at her side.

"Hi, Mom."

She looked uncertain, saying nothing. She had always been uncomfortable with greetings.

Don felt, rather than heard, Diane's intake of breath at the same moment that he saw the gun. "Mom, what the hell have you got?

Where did that come from?" He started to move forward, arm outstretched to take the gun from her.

She laughed, waving the gun toward the house, starting to say that 'Bella had found it in a box, that she wanted him to get rid of it; but the look on Don's face stopped her, and suddenly she was very afraid. All she could say was, "Donny, no!"

As Don leaped toward her she shrank back against the porch railing, involuntarily pointing the gun. When the rotting railing gave way, the old woman staggered. Falling, her hand clamped into a fist, the finger over the trigger tightening. The gun fired, spinning the woman around, a bullet plowing into Don's chest.

They all fell, the old woman in a heap, her son spread-eagled, backward, knocking his wife to the ground behind him.

Marie, who had been watching from her kitchen window, screamed. She started for the door, reconsidered, and dialed the Sheriff. From next door she could hear the old woman begin to wail.

〰〰

When the deputy arrived he found them, the man drenched in blood, dying, the old woman and the younger woman sitting, stunned, on the ground. The younger woman clutched the gun, having picked it up when Don's mother dropped it. The old woman looked up.

"I don't know what happened. It just went off. I didn't think it worked – didn't know there were bullets in it. I just wanted to give it to him, so he could take it away."

Diane climbed to her feet, stumbled to her car, and got numbly into the passenger's seat, as if waiting to go home.

A small crowd began to gather. The deputy shook his head and, lifting the old woman to her feet, carried her toward the patrol car.

Marie came to the patrol car, reached in and, not knowing what to say, clasped Ruth's hand. Ruth looked up at her. "I just wanted to give the gun to Donny. I wanted him to take it away. I was afraid."

As the patrol car pulled away, the old woman began to wail again.

Old Arthur

The thing of it was, I didn't *have* to go see old Arthur Fields to give him that discharge certificate. I could have just mailed it to him, since the damn thing had been laying around my office for weeks before I took it to him, as it was.

I didn't even have to get the early discharge for him in the first place — he still had two years on parole. Who knows how things might have been different if I hadn't been in Watts on that fateful Friday in August?

I was a PO for the California Department of Corrections in 1965, a job where I had to keep track of guys released on parole from prisons like San Quentin and Folsom and a bunch of other places you've probably never heard of.

I became a PO pretty much by accident. I had run into a guy who worked as a PO, and when I learned that he made fifty dollars a month more than I did as a bank cashier, I ran down and took the civil service test. I didn't expect to pass, since I didn't know a damn thing about corrections, but I've always been a good test-taker, and the next thing I knew a telegram came offering me a job. I was the new PO in the West LA Office of the Adult Parole Division before I could ask myself what the hell I was going to be doing chasing a bunch of ex-cons who scared the bejesus out of me.

Surprisingly, I managed to handle the job okay, learning the ins and outs, such as how to write reports and stay out of trouble and even make arrests. After three years, as a sort of promotion-without-pay, I was given an "Intensive" caseload, only 36 cases instead of the usual 70 plus. The downside was that it was in Watts.

Most of my new parolees had committed pretty serious stuff and had to be seen every week. But Arthur Fields, a no-problem parolee that helped make an otherwise difficult caseload more manageable, had been kept on the caseload by the previous PO.

Arthur was serving a sentence of 20 to 30 years for 2nd degree murder, resulting from a drunken argument in which his wife broke her neck after being pushed (or having fallen, according to Arthur) down a flight of stairs. By the time Arthur awoke from his own drunken stupor and found her at the bottom of the stairs the next morning, she was dead.

Arthur did the time, figuring that he was pretty much responsible anyway, as he was the one who had brought home the whisky. For that matter, he had started the argument; and besides, he was the one (according to his story) that left her ranting at the top of the stairs and went to bed. He did twelve years in San Quentin, and had been on parole for the past six.

If he stayed out of trouble, which, as far as I knew, Arthur always did, he would be routinely discharged from parole in two more years. I was just trying to do something decent, reward him by getting him off early, maybe as a way of making up for all the other guys I had been sending back to prison. So, I wrote a report asking for an early discharge, telling the Parole Board how Arthur was a stand-up guy who had only made this one mistake in his life.

The Board bought it, and now Arthur was off parole, only he didn't know it yet. Which was why I was planning to stop by his place on my way to the office on that hot August morning.

I had fallen out of bed at 6 AM, done all the morning things — putting on a white shirt, the pants to my brown suit, and a striped tie — and had poured myself some cereal before going out front for the morning *Times*. As I shoveled Cheerios into my mouth I did my usual newspaper review, glancing at the front-page headlines: more heat expected, another "rights" march in Alabama, LBJ sending more troops to Viet Nam, a disturbance in South Central.

Since South Central was my area I glanced over that story. Two Highway Patrol officers had chased speeders into a neighborhood and a few dozen angry citizens gathered as they made the arrest. The LAPD came out, a few more locals were arrested, and order was restored. Since I didn't recognize any of the names as parolees, I went on to the important sections: the sports — the Dodgers won again — and the funnies. I have never been able to start a day without the funnies.

Ten minutes later I threw my briefcase across the front seat of my state-issued Studebaker Lark, wishing one more time for a better car. PO's covering Watts got the worst cars in the fleet. They were still "undercover" (no "Diamond E" state license plates), but everybody knew they were "state cars." Who else would drive a Lark, for crying out loud? They were ugly as sin, overgrown kiddy-cars that you had to pedal like the devil to get up to speed for the freeways. And God forbid you should go through a puddle on a rainy day — which, fortunately, did not happen all that often in LA — because you sure as hell were going to lose your brakes.

But, the cars were free, a perk of the job, as they say, with a credit card for gas, so I tried to be grateful. Even though we weren't supposed to drive them for personal business, everybody did, so I didn't have to own a car, which was a big savings. Besides, it was probably better that all the bad guys knew who I was. That way they stayed out of my way, which was fine by me. I wanted to avoid all the trouble I could.

So, as I headed west on Century across the old Metro tracks, and ran down Alameda to take a right on 103rd, I was glad nobody was up and around. 103rd was the main east-west street in Watts,

23

primarily because it was a through street. Where a few small businesses — a grocery, hardware store, and laundromat — once stood were now empty lots, collapsed or burned-out buildings, and an empty field posing as a park. And, testimony to the area's reputation, one small building serving as an LAPD substation.

Most people called all of South-central LA "Watts," but in truth the name referred to a small residential area nestled in the southeastern corner of the city. Although the heart of LA's black community, by the standards of eastern cities Watts was an upscale ghetto. On the surface, the area's small, single family stucco homes looked no different than those of all-white Lynwood, to the east, or Compton, to the south. Beneath the surface, however, was abject poverty: no local businesses, other than a few white-owned chain stores on Central Avenue, the district's western edge; limited public transportation; little access to jobs. In far-flung LA, spread out over more than fifty square miles, a car — even a Lark — was essential for any kind of job. Few houses in Watts, even with their fenced-in yards, had garages.

I headed west on 103rd, past the police substation, and parked in front of the Regency, a dingy four-story apartment building a half-block away. Between the two buildings stood a boarded-up house, an empty lot, and a burned-out building that had been a small grocery until a year earlier. I glanced in the rear-view mirror and, seeing nobody, cut the engine, cursing under my breath as it dieseled on as usual.

While the Lark coughed into silence I rummaged through my briefcase for Arthur's discharge certificate, glancing at his file in my field book. Locking the car, I noticed, for the first time, a half-dozen men in a heated discussion on the next corner. Anybody on the streets of Watts at 8:30 in the morning was unusual; a scene like this felt ominous. I could hear raised voices, and a short, stocky man was brandishing a baseball bat and gesturing emphatically. I thought briefly about driving back to the police station to check out what was going on, but decided instead to ignore the questions rattling around in my head and just run into the building. After all, it would only take a couple of minutes to drop off the discharge.

Arthur Fields' apartment was on the third floor. The Regency was one of the taller building in Watts, but it was really pretty basic: four four-room apartments on each of four floors, stucco walls, naked light bulbs in the halls, no elevators. The rent was pretty low, making it affordable for people like Arthur, trying to make it on Social Security and odd jobs, and other single men there between prison sentences or until they could get jobs and afford nicer places.

The first time I had visited Arthur he had shown me through his apartment. Having lived in the building for several years, he had graduated into a front apartment, facing south onto 103rd. Arthur had ushered me into his living room and pointed to a slightly worn blue and gray sofa. "Found that at Goodwill; twelve dollars, and they delivered." I pushed on a lumpy cushion. "Those blue chairs — one came from a guy downstairs who was moving out, and the other I found at Sally Army. Match pretty good."

An old TV sat on an old table in the corner, and a wooden shelving unit, piled with books — I noticed Hemingway, Baldwin, a Richard Wright — was near one of two windows. A smaller table with a wooden chess board stood across the room, beside one of the blue chairs. "Found the board in a pawn shop on Central. Two dollars; only missing one horse." All four knights were on the board. Picking one up, I looked at Arthur. He shrugged. "Found a match in a shop on Central." I decided not to ask whether he had paid for it.

A small air conditioner, taken over when one of Arthur's neighbors was arrested, filled the bottom half of one window. A worn blue and gray braided oval rug, which Arthur said he carried home

25

from a used furniture store, covered the center part of the living room floor. "Five dollars," he said.

Through the living room was a narrow kitchen, clean, just barely big enough for a small table to be pushed against the end wall. One window looked west, a second faced 103rd Street. "I keeps an eye on things at the station-house," Arthur had said, pointed toward the police station, where several black-and-white LAPD squad cars were visible at the rear of the building. A bathroom and two bedrooms were accessible through a hall off the living room to the left. "Use the back one 'cause it got a window. Other room is full of junk. Gets pretty hot in there."

I had found Arthur, a slender dark-skinned man who looked younger than his 70 years, to be an interesting old man on that earlier visit, thoughtful and soft-spoken. I don't suppose he really liked me all that much; after all, I was "the man," his parole officer, and young and white to boot. But he was always polite, and as I said had never caused any trouble. So, I was looking forward to giving him his discharge in person as I approached his third-floor door.

I had just raised my hand to knock when the door flew opened, revealing a startled Arthur Fields, hat in hand, apparently on his way out. We both jumped, surprised. Arthur then leaned through the doorway, eyes darting down the hall both ways and, in a harsh whisper snarled, "Carlyle! What the hell you doing here?" He started to back into the apartment, nostrils flaring. "Git! Git on out of here, now!"

I took a step backward myself, surprised, when footsteps and loud voices rose from the rear stairwell. Arthur, looking panicked, grabbed my shirt and pulled me roughly into his apartment.

"Hey!" I yelled, preparing to assert whatever PO authority I could muster, when Arthur clapped a large black hand over my mouth.

"Jesus H. Christ, man, don't you read the damn papers?" I was about to say something clever about only reading the important parts, like the sports and the funnies, when Arthur, crossing the room to the window, continued. "It's about to blow out there, man! This whole place probably be ashes by noon!"

"What are you talking about, Arthur?" I started across the living room. "Nothing's going to happen here. There's a goddamned police station next door!"

Peering over Arthur's shoulder I saw the group of men from the corner gathering around the Lark. I watched as they circled, peering in one window after another. As if on cue the man with the baseball bat approached and, like a carnival strong-man swinging a sledge hammer, brought the bat in excruciating slow motion over his head and smashing into the windshield. The window exploded into a thousand shards of glass sparkling in the morning sun, and the group, growing in numbers, began to rock the car from side to side.

I leaned past Arthur to open the window when he shoved me aside. "Dammit, kid," he hissed, "you don't get it, do you? What the hell you thinks gonna happen to you if they find you here? You think they don't know that's a state car?"

A louder crashing sound was followed by a cheer. I peered around the edge of the window. More men had materialized, and the Lark was now on its side, it's front and rear windows broken, glass scattered on the street. One or two men were pounding on the passenger-side windows with rocks. Smashing the windows, a small man wearing a torn sleeveless undershirt reached in, pulled the door up, and dropped into the driving area.

Out flew contents: coffee travel cup, map book, briefcase, even the field book. Probably looking for a gun, I thought. Finding none — departmental rules prohibited weapons — he held a match to some loose papers from the glove box, and then dropped the burning papers into the car as he pulled himself out.

A big, shirtless man caught the field book and began leafing through pages. Shit!" I said, under my breath. Information, records — even mug shots — and case notes on some thirty-five parolees, including Arthur Fields, were in that book. Two or three men, standing near him, turned to look at the Regency, appearing to focus on Arthur's window. "Shit!" I said again. Or was that Arthur?

To be honest, I'm not too sure in what order things happened after that. I saw several men start up the steps into the building while flames and smoke began to billow out of the car. I looked around the room frantically, finally fixing on Arthur, who was staring at me.

"Lord shit a'mighty," he said, mixing profanity in a way that made perfect sense. "They find you here both our asses' be fried." Grabbing my arm, he began pulling me, half running and half staggering, toward the unused bedroom. Flinging open the closet door he shoved me in saying, through clenched teeth, "Git in there! Hide yo' white ass!"

I fell into a pile of clothes as he shoved the door shut. Darkness and mustiness closed in on me as I tried to burrow beneath the pile. I could hear shouting, footsteps in the hall, fists pounding on doors. A muffled explosion seemed to shake the building. The Lark's gas tank? As my eyes adjusted I slid behind a stack of boxes at the side of the closet, pulling clothes from the floor and the hanging rod over me and huddled in the corner, soaked with sweat and shaking with fear.

I could hear Arthur arguing with someone, the words getting clearer as the voices neared. "What the fuck, Jeremy, you think I'd hide JC in here? What kind of fool you think I am?"

"JC," street slang for a parole officer, as in, "Naw, I can't come over tonight, baby, I think JC be comin' by!" JC, because POs were supposed to be as powerful as Jesus Christ. I didn't feel much like JC right now, I thought, huddled in a dark closet under a pile of dirty clothes.

"That white dude's around somewhere, old man! Ain't nobody else home. Ain't you on parole?"

"Naw, man! Got me a discharge in yonder. Got off early. I never did see no PO much. I jest tries to be peaceable."

"Well, old man, we look around anyhow. You never know — he might have slipped in here whilst yo' back was turned."

A line of light, visible through a crack between boxes, appeared under the closet door as a light came on in the room. Suddenly the closet was filled with light as the door was opened. Crouching into as small a space as possible, I held my breath, trying to quiet my pounding heart.

"Jesus, old man, you got clothes in here as old as sin! Don't you never throw anything away?" A bearded face appeared above me as old coats and shirts were parted, and a hand pushed me roughly in the side. "Even piles of old clothes and shit on the floor! You git's the housekeeper of the year award, old man!" The younger man laughed, slamming the door shut. "Don't really matter much, you hear? Best you clear out anyway — this place be torched pretty soon."

I could hear Arthur arguing as they moved away. "Why you wanna do that? This my home, man. Ain't got no place else to live. Why y'all burn me out?"

"Ain't you, old man. It's Whitey. We burnin' Whitey."

Their voices became muffled, and I thought I heard the apartment's hallway door slam shut. In the distance, approaching sirens — fire engines and police cars. I could hear popping sounds. Gunshots? The Lark was attracting a crowd.

Arthur was gone for what seemed to be hours, but was probably only a few minutes. I could hear the fire truck pulling away, and could pick up whiffs of pungent, oil-fired smoke mixing with the closet's musty old-clothes smells. I was afraid to leave my safe haven, such as it was, but hiding in a burning building didn't seem like a very good idea either. And where the hell was Arthur, anyway? Out telling Jeremy where I was?

Unsure what to do, unable to make a decision of any kind, I remained crouched in the corner of the closet, becoming more and more uncomfortable. One by one, muscles I didn't know I had began to scream. Plus, I was soaked with sweat. Pretty soon, I figured, they could find me with their noses, as I struggled to shed my suit coat under the pile of clothing.

I was peeking out of the closet door, still undecided and exhausted, when Arthur returned. Without my realizing it, things had grown quiet.

"Still here, Carlyle? I was hopin' you'd took off." No smile; teeth clenched. "Best we gets you out of there whilst you can still unfold."

Looking around nervously, I followed Arthur into the kitchen. I sat at the table, numbly trying to regain my senses.

"Where were you?"

Arthur just looked at me.

"What'll I do if they come back?"

"They won't, least wise for a while," he said, looking out the window. "Last I heard most of 'ems headed for Central, fixin' to burn stores." He looked back at me. "If they does, you knows where to hide."

"What about this place? Won't they burn this building?"

"Maybe. Maybe not. Think this building's owned by a brother runs a funeral parlor over on Crenshaw. Anyways, I tried to talk Jeremy into leaving it be." Anything but certain.

"Central Avenue? Maybe I can get out of here."

Arthur looked out at the street. "Ain't nobody wants you gone more'n me, Carlyle, but you wouldn't git ten feet out there." He smiled then, surprisingly. "Besides, your little car ain't too drivable right now."

I looked out the window, taking a minute to realize that the burned and crumpled heap in front of the building was what was left of my Lark. "Jesus!" I moaned, shaking my head. "My supervisor will have my ass!"

"Wasn't really much of a car, Carlyle," Fields said, shaking his head. "That little Lark sho-nuff deserved to die. Besides, how many cars can say they set off a riot?"

I looked at Arthur, trying to find humor in his face, before recognizing the distant sounds of sirens, shouting and gunshots. I looked out the window again, toward the west, finally registering the glow of fires and drifting smoke.

Arthur went into the living room and turned on the TV. First reports of a developing riot were coming on. Store burnings on Central Avenue, gunfire, cars overturned and set on fire. No shit, I thought.

Through the kitchen window I could see groups of men running down 103rd. I sat, drenched and drained, staring numbly for half an hour before it occurred to me to look out the kitchen's other window. "Arthur," I called to my reluctant host still in the living room, "why can't I just run over to the police station?"

Arthur came into the kitchen, and pointed toward a house across 103rd. I could see faces in two or three windows, and another man sitting cross-legged on the flat roof. A sun-generated glint disclosed the rifle, lying across his lap. "Cops under siege, Carlyle. They on the roof of this building too, I 'spect. Po-lice probably got the door barricaded. They in worse shape than you."

"You've got to be kidding me. This is LA — why the hell haven't they come in with tanks?"

"Don't know if the LAPD has tanks. TV says the Mayor's askin' Reagan to call out the National Guard."

"What the hell do I do in the meantime? The longer I stay here, the worse it is."

"Don't know what you can do about that." Arthur looked more uncertain than he sounded, but said, "Maybe you be okay for a while."

Going to the refrigerator, Arthur pulled lunch meat and sliced cheese out, along with mustard and bread. "Guess if I's stuck with you, might as well git you somethin' to eat." Digging in a cabinet, he dumped a can of soup into a pot. The aroma of the warming soup began to stir an appetite.

"You know, Carlyle," Arthur said as he poured tomato soup into a bowl, "it ain't that I don't 'preciate what you done for me. You jest picked a hell of a bad time to show up."

"Wasn't the brightest move of my week, Arthur."

I looked out the window. Fires were burning down the street, smoke billowing past the window. Shifting groupings of men moved around the street, calling to one another, gesturing angrily.

"I think you may need another place to live, Arthur."

Arthur glanced out the window, frowning. "Maybe I can buy me a place with the reward money I'll get for saving your white ass. Or sellin' it."

I looked at him, hoping the last part was a joke. "I don't know how much a lousy PO's white ass is worth, Arthur."

We moved into the living room, and I sat on the couch watching the riot coverage on television. Scattered fires were burning along the commercial strips on Central and Crenshaw, the Fire Department not responding because of sniper fire. There were reports of widespread looting. A report of a rumored march on Lynwood caught my attention.

"I sure as hell wish you had a phone, Arthur."

"Never needed one. Don't have anybody left to call," he said. Realizing that I'd seen no pictures or signs of anyone else in Arthur's life, I figured he was referring to his dead wife.

"You miss her, Arthur? After all this time?"

"Sometimes. She was a good 'nuf woman. Drank too much, but so did I back then. She sure as hell didn't deserve to die."

More reports: fires, gunfire, sometimes on TV, sometimes outside in the street. Police arrests now totaling thirty, according to the reports; seventeen known dead. Watching, I finally had to ask. "Why here, Arthur? There are lots of worse places to live than Watts."

He thought for a bit before responding. "You wouldn't say that if you lived here, Carlyle. Everythin's relative. Everybody lives in a rat hole, you don't feel so bad. But you fence people in, even in a nice enough place, let them see what they can't have that other folks got, they get riled up."

"But why burn your own places down?"

"You fenced in, what else you got to burn?"

Hours crawled. Once or twice footsteps in the hall led me to scramble back into the closet, huddled and shivering. But no one else came to the door and hiding served little purpose other than enabling me to retrieve my wadded-up coat and tie. The riot, while growing in intensity, seemed to remain several blocks away.

"You a chess player, Carlyle?"

"A little." Actually, I barely knew how to move the pieces.

Fields pulled the chess table over to the couch, got a chair from the kitchen, and moved the white king's pawn two spaces. It was a strange scene, an old, neatly dressed, black man and a young, disheveled, white man playing chess while sirens approached and departed, scenes of rioting played on the television, and a barricaded police station lay under siege next door.

Arthur whipped me three straight games.

Every once in a while, waiting for me to move, I'd see Arthur looking at me, eyes narrowed. Once or twice he got up to look out of a window. He seemed to be trying to work something out.

About 6:30 Arthur got up, stretched, picked up his hat, and announced he was going out. "Goin' to look around," he said. "Anybody come around, you knows where to hide."

Alone in the apartment I felt even more trapped. Almost immediately I heard footsteps. I scrambled back into the closet, frozen with fear. Huddled in the closet, my mind raced through one unworkable escape option after another. As time passed, the paranoia kept at bay while Arthur had been there intensified. Where the hell was he, anyway? Probably figured he stood a better chance of getting rewarded for turning me over to the rioters. What did he expect — that I would just sit here until he made his deal and came back for me?

As my fear turned into anger I emerged from the closet, returning into the kitchen. I looked out the window at the police station. The only ways in were through the front, on 103rd, or through a rear door. My chances of getting to either door was slim, and even slimmer that anyone inside would open one up. I was sitting in a frying pan, surrounded by fire. And I was being protected by an old black man who was probably out selling my white ass at that very moment.

As it began to grow dark I decided to run. It was only a few blocks, less than a mile, to Alameda. I could run that far. I was looking out the window, trying to decide on a route, when I heard a key in the door.

I looked around frantically, trying to find something to swing or throw. Nothing – Arthur was much too neat.

Arthur walked in, carrying my scorched briefcase. Assessing the look on my face, he said, "Be cool, Carlyle. You almost home." He tossed the briefcase on the couch. "But you'd best move away from that window. I could see you for two blocks."

34

"I'm getting out of here, Arthur," I said, voice rising in panic. "I'm going to make a break for it."

"No, you ain't. You wouldn't get a block out there. I ain't holin' you up all day and then lettin' you git killed out there."

Anger overwhelmed the panic. "So, what the hell do you propose, Arthur? That I just sit here until this all dies down? Or till Watts burns down?" I looked at him. "Or maybe until you sell me out?"

"Be cool, man," Arthur said again. "You be out of here in a couple of hours, after it's good and dark."

"How the hell am I going to do that, Arthur? Paint me a black face?"

"I said, be cool, Carlyle!" Arthur's voice was raised, demanding. "You ain't going nowhere on your own!" He started for the kitchen, then stopped. "You being a PO ain't worth shit now, Carlyle. I's your only hope here. I wants to sell you out, I sells you out. Probably what I oughts to do." He went into the kitchen, emerging with a glass of water. "But I ain't goin' do that. I ain't goin' stand 'round and let somebody else die 'cause I didn't do nothin'." He took a drink of water. "I's goin' take care of it. Then I won't have to see your white ass no more."

I slumped onto the couch. "Jesus, Arthur, I'm sorry. I'm just scared shitless, is all."

"It be okay, Carlyle. You be home to Lynwood soon." Did Arthur know where I lived? Of course, my address was in the telephone book. Departmental policy, for some asinine reason.

Exhausted and defeated, with no workable alternative plan, I looked at Arthur. "OK. What's your plan?"

No response. Arthur went back into the kitchen and stood, looking out toward the police station.

"Shit, Arthur," I said, returning my attention to the TV. "I don't care how you do it. Just get me out of here." I spent the next two hours in a stupor, staring at the tube, watching "continuing coverage" of fires, looting and threats.

About nine-thirty Arthur went in his bedroom and changed into black pants and a black shirt, and emerged carrying a black knit cap and gloves. "Wait here. You hear two toots on a car horn, you hustle down the back steps. But be careful, you hear? Anybody around, stay here. I'll circle around and be back."

Before I could protest he was gone. I got up, turned off the TV, and went into the kitchen. Shifting from window to window I peered into the darkness, more panicked by the minute. Arthur was going to get Jeremy for sure now. I was dead meat. I needed to take care of things myself, make a run for it. Better to die running than be executed. Or burned.

As I returned to "make a break for it" scenarios, I noticed a squad car, lights off, moving slowly down the alley behind the police station. It nosed alongside the building in the parking lot, and two uniformed cops emerged. Crouching low, they scurried toward the building. Must have radioed they were coming. Reinforcements? Or preparing to evacuate?

I thought about running over, pounding on the door, getting someone to let me in. Probably wouldn't work, I decided. If I was in there I'd sure as hell shoot first before asking who was there.

I was on my own.

Deciding finally to run, I put on my crumpled coat and picked up the briefcase. Then, realizing they would only make me more of a target, I threw them back on the couch. Opening the apartment's door, I was looking carefully up and down the hall when I heard a car horn.

Two beats.

It was now or never.

The building seemed empty. Not surprising, I thought, since all the excitement was outside. Heart pounding, I crept down the back steps and looked carefully out the window of the door to the alley.

There, in the alley, lights off and motor running, was a "black and white," an LAPD police car.

I raced out the door, relief flooding through me. As I approached the squad car, however, I stopped short: sitting low in the driver's seat, knit cap pulled down over his face, almost invisible in the shadows, was Arthur Fields.

"Popped the trunk, Carlyle," he whispered. "Get in and pull it shut."

"What the shit? Where the hell did you get a police car, Arthur?"

"Get in the trunk. We ain't got all night here."

"Right, Arthur. Then what? Where are you fixing to drive me?"

"Get your white ass in the trunk, Carlyle," Fields hissed, nervously, "'fore you gits us both killed."

Looking around frantically, trying to decide which direction to run, I suddenly heard voices from above: "Hey, man — you hear sumptin? Somebody down there?"

I got in, pulling the trunk lid down after me.

"Slam it shut." I was surprised how clearly, I could hear his voice.

Slamming the lid locked I shouted, "Where'd you get this, Arthur?"

Instead of responding, he put the car in gear and began to drive, slowly at first, then more rapidly. We turned a corner, then several more, before bouncing over something rough. Railroad tracks? A moment later the car stopped, and the trunk lid popped open.

"Git out, Carlyle. You on your own now."

Clambering out, I realized we were on an isolated side street on the Lynwood side of Alameda. I leaned in the passenger side window.

"How did you manage this, you old bastard?"

"Been watchin' 'em ever since it got dark — slippin' in off the alley, into the station-house. Figure they watchin' out front, ain't payin' no mind to the back." Arthur looked at me, anticipating my next question. "What the hell — you think I don't know how to hot-wire? They's a lot you don't know, Carlyle."

"I sure as hell see that, Arthur." I thought for a minute. "How are you going to get it back? You think nobody'll notice an old guy driving a black and white?"

"Ain't intendin' to drive it. Ditch it t'other side of Alameda. An old black guy blends in, Carlyle." Arthur glanced around, checked the rear-view mirror. "Git on now. You on your own turf."

The immensity of the thing he had done for me hit me then. "Jesus, Arthur, how can I ever thank you?"

"You already did, Carlyle. It's in my pocket." He put the car in gear. "Fact is, that discharge probably saved yo' ass. I showed it to Jeremy to convince him I warn't on parole no more. Good thing you let it lay 'round 'for bringin' it out.'"

Before I could say anything else he had peeled away, rounding the corner back toward Alameda.

As I had anticipated, my supervisor was not pleased with the loss of the Lark, but I was more royally reamed for having gone to Watts in the first place.

"Don't you read the damned newspaper, Carlyle?"

"Just the important parts. The sports and funnies."

"This isn't funny, Carlyle. You could have been killed. Jesus," he said, peering over his glasses with only the smallest of smiles, "think of the paperwork!"

As it turned out, I didn't get fired, and I didn't even have to pay for the car, which was replaced by a Dodge Dart. In fact, I actually got promoted, to Assistant Supervisor, a few months later. I was always a good test-taker.

Of course, my story followed me. I've been forever known as the PO who lost a Lark in the Watts Riots. Fortunately, nobody knew how much it was involved in setting the riot off in the first place.

I drove down 103rd a few weeks after the riots, after we were allowed back into Watts, hoping to thank Arthur properly. The Regency was a pile of rubble, having burned, I learned, about midnight on the first day of the rioting. The fire department had been called, but fearing snipers, had refused to respond.

Arthur's name never did show up — not on any death list, or arrest list, or any other list. I checked over several months but could never find an address or phone number. It was as if he had never existed. I still think of him, of course, every once in a while, hoping against hope that he made it through, that he found a "peaceable" place to live out his remaining years.

The Affair

Reggie Arnold was 42 years old and in his third August as minister of the First Community Church of Spring City when he concluded that he was in love with his church organist.

He did not come to this decision lightly. Reggie was, as far as he knew, a happily married man with three beautiful (if sometimes noisy) young daughters. Furthermore, his ministry was coming along: the congregation was beginning to respond to his leadership, and Sunday morning attendance was growing. At first, therefore, he just attributed his feelings to lust.

Reggie had always been able to see Kathy Leighter at the organ as he sat behind the pulpit on Sunday mornings, but he only gradually realized what he was watching while she played. When he recognized that he was staring at her legs — revealed as her fashionable knee-length skirts rose up her thigh — or her breasts pressing against her crisp white blouses while she stretched and reached, he was mortified.

For two Sunday mornings after this discovery Reggie scrupulously avoided looking at Kathy. As compensation, or perhaps atonement, he paid more attention to his wife, Lillian. Still, his need to avoid thinking about Kathy, and the effort required to do it, somehow made everything worse. He was a mess — confused, guilty, and — if only he could have admitted it — angry.

In retrospect, of course, it should have been easy to see that something was wrong. His sermons, usually a strong point with the congregation, were flat and confusing as he stumbled with distraction. He missed — forgot — meetings. He snapped at people

41

— his secretary Arlene Wright, church board members, Lillian, even Kathy — that he normally would have carefully attended. And he was unable to look anyone in the eyes, not his secretary, board members, Lillian, or especially Kathy.

Lillian, of course, did notice. Wary, even if flattered by the increased attention, Lillian asked one evening if anything was wrong. Reggie responded defensively: "Of course not. No. Why do you ask?" Distracted by a crying child, Lilly let the matter drop.

Kathy, of course, had known she was being watched with that sixth sense women have. She was certainly flattered — her husband Rob had ignored her for years — and she had come to admire Reggie during the six months she had worked as organist at First Church, but she was also confused. Her senses told her that Reggie was attracted to her, but he was such a good, caring man that she was sure she must be misreading the signs.

Kathy had lived in Spring City less than a year, having been transferred from Capital City to a supervisory position with the state's Accounting and Auditing Division. She had not wanted to move — her aging parents were in Capital City and she knew no one in Spring City — but it was a promotion and they had needed the money because Rob had such difficulty holding a job. Besides, on a career "fast-track," she anticipated being back in Capital City in a year or two.

She had sought work as a church organist — music was her first love — because the part-time position offered a little extra money as well as some evening and weekend activities. Life with Rob — who was seldom home and largely uninvolved even when he was there — was lonely at best.

So, Kathy decided to trust Reggie. He was, after all, a man of God, who would never allow anything bad to happen. So, she was not really conscious that she was wearing more appealing outfits to church on Sunday mornings, or that she was sending reinforcing nonverbal signals back to him, smiling when she caught him looking, moving a little more revealingly when she played.

Reggie could not continue his self-imposed abstinence, of course, and when Kathy wore the tight pink skirt that struck just above her knees and the crisp white lacy blouse he stared like a love-struck adolescent. Nevertheless, his sermon was surprisingly enlivened, and Kathy, ever observant, played with particular vigor. Most of the congregation was also thrilled: finally, after all these weeks, a worship service with spirit!

But Lilly, uncertain and concerned, continued to worry.

Typically, Reggie kept a fairly regular schedule: off on Mondays, hospital and pastoral calls Tuesday through Friday mornings, luncheons and other meetings throughout the week, committee and board meetings Tuesday, Wednesday and Thursday evenings. In addition, he was compulsive about working out, exercising at the gym three afternoons each week. Although he would work on his sermons as he had time during the week, that work usually consisted of research; his pattern had always been to set aside Saturdays for actual sermon preparation.

Lillian had come to accept this pattern even though it left her with the lion's share of home and child care. A school teacher, she worked long hours herself. She had never wanted to be a minister's wife, but she knew how important it was to Reggie, and that he invested everything he had into his church. Besides, his evening work gave her time to prepare for lessons and grade papers.

But Lilly did not teach during the summer, and she had increasingly complained in recent years about Reggie's Saturday sermon preparation. Like most ministers Reggie was usually exhausted by Sunday afternoon; Saturday was the only day they could possibly have together.

So, it seemed reasonable enough when Reggie offered to change his schedule and stay later at church Wednesday and Thursday evenings to write his sermons. Certainly, staying at the church made sense: a house full of active children and an interrupting wife are not conducive to sermon preparation. The fact that Wednesday evening was also the scheduled time for choir practice was almost, but not quite, coincidental.

So, Reggie should not have been startled, which he was, when Kathy stopped at his office door after choir practice one Wednesday evening. He dropped his pen when he saw her, recovered nicely, and said, "Oh, hello! Can I help you?"

Kathy had, in fact, almost passed by Reggie's office, and then had stood, hand raised, for several moments before knocking. But she was lonely, and she needed someone to talk with. Finally, resolved, she tapped on the door.

"I was just leaving and saw your light on. Do we need to discuss Sunday's music?" It was the best excuse she could come up with; she and Reggie seldom discussed the worship service music. Reggie's pattern was to select hymns to fit his topic, while Kathy made her own decisions about preludes, postludes and choir anthems.

Reggie could hear choir members leaving, calling out to one another as doors slammed and cars started up. "No, I don't suppose." Then, after a moment's frantic reflection: "Well, yes, we probably should. Why don't you come in?"

Kathy sat on the office love seat, crossing her legs demurely. Reggie shuffled papers on his desk, finally finding the service outline he usually faxed to her on Thursdays. "Here's the outline. Have you been able to work from what I've been sending?"

"Oh, yes. It's been working fine." An awkward pause. "Has my playing been all right?"

"Good heavens yes!" Reggie could feel beads of sweat on his brow. "Everyone seems very pleased."

Kathy smiled, settled back into the couch. Reggie, realizing that everyone else had left and that they were alone in the church, also began to relax. "How's Rob?"

She frowned. "I don't know. He's drinking more than ever. And he's lost his job again." Failing to compose herself, Kathy began to cry. Feeling compassion, Reggie moved around the desk and sat beside her.

"That's got to be difficult for you. I'm so sorry. I wish I could help."

"I know. It is, sometimes. You do, really. I just . . ."

A door slammed somewhere in the building. Both started, and Kathy rose to move toward the door. "I'd better leave. Thanks for listening."

Reggie followed her to the office door. "Anytime, Kathy. Feel free to stop in or call if there is anything I can do. Or just to talk."

Kathy reached out, touching Reggie's arm. "Thanks," she said, softly, before turning and walking swiftly down the hall.

Reggie followed Kathy with his eyes before returning to his desk. But he could not concentrate on his sermon, so after a few moments he gathered his things and left for home.

On the way out, Reggie wondered who was in the building, but then he noticed the janitor's car in the parking lot. "He must be working late this evening," he thought, as he allowed his mind to drift back to images of Kathy — working the organ, touching his arm, walking down the hall. By the time he reached home he was agitated and alarmed.

He was relieved to see that Lilly had already gone to bed, and he sat in the kitchen for a few moments composing himself before following her.

★

Kathy Leighter was relieved when, pulling into the parking area near her apartment, she saw that Rob's car was not in its usual space. She did not want to have to contend with Rob's brooding presence tonight.

Kathy felt good, surprisingly exhilarated, after her brief talk with Pastor Reggie. He was such a good, caring man, one of the few men with whom she felt safe. As she walked into the apartment she glanced at the clock. Nearly ten: with luck she could be asleep before Rob came home from the bar.

She feigned sleep when he came home thirty minutes later. It was a tactic she often used; she could not stand to talk with him, much less have him touch her, when he had been drinking.

Rob actually had come home early, having drunk relatively less than usual — and only coffee the last two hours — while he brooded alone in a corner booth of the bar. He certainly knew that Kathy had been angry, especially after he had lost his job. But that jerk of a foreman, Gerard, had made it impossible to stay there, baiting him constantly. Still, Rob wanted things to be better with Kathy. If Kathy could be happy, he thought, then he could get out and get another job.

For two hours as he sat in the bar Rob had gone over in his mind what he might say to Kathy, how he might make it better. A little after ten, still unclear about what he would say, he left, intending to get home before she went to bed... When he walked into the apartment, though, and found the lights out, his mood immediately darkened.

Rob puttered around in the kitchen for a few minutes, considering whether to wake Kathy up. But he didn't want to do anything to make her angrier; and he was never sure lately what would or would not make things worse. Finally, hurt and disappointed, he tiptoed into the bedroom, took off his clothes, and got into the bed.

Kathy was lying on her side facing away from Rob, knees pulled up to her chest. Although she was breathing regularly he was unsure if she was asleep, so he reached a hand and touched her lightly on the hip. "You awake, Kath?"

She said nothing, but her breath stopped for a moment and he could sense her body stiffening. He pulled away, hurt, and almost immediately began to feel anger rising. "I know you're awake, Kathy," he said.

When she did not respond he reached over again, moving his hand down her leg from her hip to her knee. She pulled her leg away even more, rolling further away from him. "Not now," she murmured; "I've got to get up early in the morning to go to work."

It was like a slap in the face, and his rage began to boil. He rolled over to his other side, facing away from Kathy, seething; and then, with a growl, rolled back and pulled her roughly onto her back. "Damn you," he said, his breath hot with the smell of stale beer, "I don't deserve to be treated this way!"

Pulling her panties down to her ankles he spread her legs apart and, climbing between them, roughly entered her. Holding her down with his weight he thrust once, twice, three times and ejaculated. His aggressiveness surprised her and, legs pinned by her underwear around her ankles, his rough entry was painful. She gasped and let out a cry. "I knew you'd like it," he mumbled, as he rolled away and faced the wall.

Kathy lay still for a long time, stunned, until she realized Rob had fallen asleep. She finally got out of bed, and after crying in the kitchen for a few minutes went into the bathroom and drew a bath. She felt dirty and humiliated and sat, shivering and crying, in the tub for a long time. Ultimately, anger surfaced. Kathy spent the remainder of the night, and several nights after that, on the living room couch.

*

Kathy did not tell anyone about Rob's attack, and gradually a tense peace settled between them. Rob, trying desperately to atone, found a job loading trucks, and made it a point to be home most evenings. As a result, he was drinking less, usually going out only on Friday evenings.

Kathy continued to stop by Reggie's office each Wednesday after choir practice, puttering around the choir room until the choir members had all left. Then, taking the long way out of the building, she would tap on his closed office door. Reggie, who always managed to appear hard at work, would put away his papers and welcome her in.

Gradually their conversations lengthened. Reggie was a good listener, a quality that served him well as a pastor; and over time Kathy revealed more of her disappointments and doubts about her marriage. Although she never said anything about Rob's attack, she did share her frustration with his erratic work history, his drinking, and what seemed to her to be his perpetual anger. More and more, she confided, she had been realizing how little they have in common.

"I suppose I should be more understanding," she said one Wednesday; "Rob did have a rotten childhood." When Reggie started to respond she continued, "I really can't stand his father. He's stopped drinking now, but he's still a scary man. And he must have been a real terror when Rob and his older brother were little — from what I hear, he could care less who he knocked around when he was drinking." Another pause, and then in a low voice Kathy said, "I'm not sure a person can ever recover from something like that."

Reggie, not knowing what to say in response, focused instead on comforting and validating Kathy. In fact, he had come to rationalize these regular meetings with her (which he had never mentioned to Lillian) as "counseling."

At first, therefore, he said little about himself. But gradually, perhaps because so much of Kathy's tone was negative, or perhaps to justify what he was doing, he began to express more and more dissatisfaction with his own marriage.

Most of the congregation saw Lillian Arnold as the perfect pastor's wife. But she was a practical woman, focused on her work, her children, and the myriad household tasks Reggie had no time for. Still, Reggie usually seemed engrossed in his work, and it did not occur to her that he might feel ignored.

And although she continued to feel a vague sense of uncertainty, she trusted Reggie. She knew he had always been a man of integrity, a quality she admired; so, she concluded that his recent distraction and increased time away from home reflected increased work demands.

After all, she certainly had her own hands full. During most of the year she held down a demanding job while still caring for Lucy, Linda and LeAnn (the three "L's" had been Reggie's idea), and keeping the household together, to say nothing of all the activities a pastor's wife was required to attend. And the summers were no better: compensating for her school-year absence she tried to spend as much time with the girls as possible.

So, Lilly Arnold chose to see her marriage as a good one, stable and secure. If she and Reggie occasionally lost track of each other, it was nothing that could not be repaired. Perhaps they could leave the girls with a church family — Arlene Wright, maybe, who the girls considered an "honorary aunt" — and get away for a weekend together.

It was on a Friday evening in September, after Reggie had come to bed hoping to make love, only to find Lilly already asleep, when things crystallized for him. Disappointment growing into anger, Reggie realized that he felt more appreciated and cared for in his

Wednesday evening meetings with Kathy than he did from his wife the rest of the week.

And on Sunday morning, when Kathy smiled at him from the organ, he decided that it was not lust; he must be falling in love with her.

Alarmed, Reggie told himself that he needed to stop things before they got out of hand, needed to keep away from Kathy and address his concerns with Lil. Wednesday evenings with Kathy had become too important, were too dangerous. Furthermore, despite their problems, he loved Lillian. And he was a pastor: he could not jeopardize his church with something like this.

But when Kathy, leaving after the service, smiled and touched his arm as she hurried down the hall, Reggie momentarily melted. By the time he got home, after attending to the various odds and ends parishioners always bring to pastors after Sunday services, he was agitated and angry. Distracted, he snapped at LeAnn, ate his lunch in silence, and then went into the bedroom for a nap.

It was not unusual for Reggie to nap after lunch on Sundays, but Lillian realized something was wrong this day. After cleaning up the kitchen she asked Lucy to watch the younger girls, saying she was also going to take a nap. As she closed the bedroom door she realized that Reggie was not asleep. As she crawled onto the bed Reggie turned away. Moving closer she reached an arm around his chest, and pulled herself closer.

"Are you tired, Hon?" It was not so much a question as an invitation, one of the ways they had come to address the possibility of sex.

"Yeah, I guess so," Reggie mumbled, ignoring the implication. "It's been a long week."

Lilly resisted the urge to say it had been a long week for her, also, and in fact a long several weeks. Instead, she pulled Reggie a little closer and held him tightly. Gradually, his resolve softened, and he turned to her.

✶

Reggie planned to talk with Kathy Wednesday evening, to tell her they had to stop meeting. But in the end, he could not. First, she was late — nearly thirty minutes after choir practice — and then she seemed distressed. Reggie, having concluded she was not coming, viewed her arrival with surprising relief.

"I could not get rid of Betty Phillips and Mary Conners," she said, angrily; "they kept on fiddling with music and the new choir robe catalogue. I thought they'd never leave." Then she smiled and said, "If they only knew how important these conversations are for me. . . ." Uncertain, she left the sentence unfinished.

"Is everything all right?" Kathy seemed unusually upset.

"No." Kathy's eyes moistened. "Everything is not all right."

It took several minutes for Reggie, back in his pastoral mode, to get Kathy to talk; and by then his own resolve had dissipated. When she began, speaking about Rob, he felt back on familiar ground, "legitimate".

"He's always so angry," Kathy finally said. "And now that he's got a job it's almost as if he thinks everything should be fine between us." She stopped short of saying anything about what had happened a few weeks ago, that made it impossible for everything to ever be all right again.

"And now that he's home most evenings it's even worse." She paused for a long moment, and then added, in a soft, rueful voice, "Last Wednesday he was furious because I was so late getting home."

Reggie felt a surge of panic and struggled to keep his composure. This was, of course, the perfect opportunity; and yet he was suddenly clear that he did not want to end it, did not want these times together to end.

"What does Rob think you're doing?"

"I don't know. I suppose he doesn't know. He asked if I were having an affair."

More panic. "But you're not! How could he think that?"

Kathy looked at Reggie. "Maybe I should. I'm going to be accused of it anyway." Then she looked away, face reddening. She began to cry.

Reggie, confused, wanted to comfort her. He moved next to her on the couch. Not knowing what to say, he took her hand in his. Kathy fumbled in her purse for a tissue but did not pull away. Drying her eyes, she looked at Reggie. "Thank you," she said. "Thanks for caring." She got up to leave, and Reggie followed her to the door. One hand on the knob, Kathy reached up and kissed him lightly on the lips. Opening the door, she fled down the hall.

Reggie sat at his desk for a long time after Kathy left, trying to sort things out. He knew he needed to stop this thing with Kathy, but he also knew he did not want to. She was becoming too important, so important that he wanted more than anything to take away her pain. But he could not bear the thought of hurting Lillian. And then there were the girls. And the church. Anguished, he finally got up to go home.

Fortunately, Lilly was asleep when he finally came to bed.

*

The next Wednesday evening Reggie mentioned that he was going to be in town on Friday. "Can you get away from your office for lunch?"

Kathy told her supervisor that she had a doctor's appointment and, a little out of breath, met Reggie at La Tosca's, a small Italian restaurant she had suggested because it was poorly lit and a little off the beaten path. In this setting their conversation became more animated, marked by frequent laughter, and even more personal. As

Kathy rose to leave, already late, she reached for Reggie's hand and, embracing him, reached up to kiss him warmly.

As Kathy ran out of the restaurant Reggie left a tip and walked to the cashier to pay the bill. The young woman at the cash register smiled, took his credit card, and asked, "Did you enjoy lunch?"

"Oh, yes," Reggie responded, smiling himself, as if they shared a special secret. "Lunch was very nice, thank you."

Over the next few weeks Reggie met Kathy for lunch once or twice a week. Usually they returned to La Tosca's, but occasionally, when Kathy could come up with no excuse giving her more than her usual 45 minutes for lunch, they met at a lunch counter near her office. Their conversations became lighter, more familiar, assuming an intimacy Reggie could never remember sharing at meals with Lillian. Reggie realized that he was happy, happier than he had been in years.

Ironically, Reggie's increasing involvement with Kathy actually seemed to improve things with Lillian. He seemed to be in a better mood, complained less about work, and was even more affectionate. Reggie began approaching Lil for sex two or three times a week, something that had not happened for years. Whatever had been bothering him, Lilly decided, he must have figured it out.

When Reggie mentioned, at lunch one day, that he was going to be out of town for a few days the next week, Kathy seemed alarmed. "It's no big deal," he said, "just a denominational training program."

"What days? Where will you be?"

"Capital City. The sessions begin early Wednesday morning, and end Thursday about three. But I'm planning to meet a seminary buddy Tuesday evening for dinner." After a pause he took her hand. "I'm really sorry I won't be here Wednesday."

Kathy smiled ruefully. "Well, you have to do what you have to do."

"Kathy," Reggie said, "I'd really rather be here with you. This training is required."

"I know," she said; but she was subdued the rest of the meal. Still, when Kathy stood to leave for her office she reached over and kissed Reggie, as usual.

"I hope everything is all right," the girl at the register said as Reggie paid the bill.

Although Reggie usually took Mondays off, he went in to the office Monday afternoon before leaving on Tuesday. Arlene, the church secretary, handed him the mail as he passed on the way to his office. "Oh," she said as he was opening her door, "do you know if anything is wrong with Kathy Leighter?"

He stopped, trying to appear casual. "No. Why?"

"She canceled choir practice this week. Said something about needing to see her parents. I think they're getting up in years — wasn't Kathy the youngest?"

Reggie realized that he did not know. "Oh? I didn't know that. I'll try to call her." As he started into his office he turned. "What will the choir do Sunday?"

"Kathy said they're singing an anthem they've sung several times before. They can get ready Sunday morning before church."

Reggie tried to call Kathy at work, but she was not available. He left a message, but she did not return his call.

Lillian seemed genuinely sad as she left for school Tuesday morning. She was running late; they had made love that morning after waking a few minutes early. "I'll miss you," she said as she kissed Reggie at the door. "See you Thursday evening."

"I should be here for dinner," Reggie called as she hurried to her car.

As Reggie drove to Capital City he worried about Kathy. Still, he was in a good mood as he greeted Andy James in the hotel dining room. He and Andy had been friends in Seminary, and had kept up with each other as their careers took them to different parts of the state. Andy currently served a church in the outskirts of Capital City.

"Wow," Andy said as they were seated. "You look great! What have you been drinking?"

Reggie laughed, and brought Andy up on how well things were going with First Church, Lil, and his kids. The only thing he omitted was Kathy.

Things were not as good with Andy, however, and the two men sat at the table, talking, for more than two hours. Finally, Andy stretched, looked at his watch, and said, "Wow! I've got to get some sleep. And I promised to get home before ten."

As Andy started for the parking garage Reggie clasped him around the shoulder. "See you in the morning. How about breakfast — about 7:30?"

"7:30," said Andy, waving as he went through the garage door.

Reggie had decided not to call Lil as he entered his room. She was usually asleep by nine, and he did not want to wake her up. "I'll call in the morning, before she leaves for school," he thought. But when he saw the blinking red light on the telephone, indicating that he had a message waiting, he thought it might be her. He called the desk and was connected with the hotel's voice mail system.

"Reggie." It was Kathy's voice. "Can you call me tonight? Please; whenever you get in." Almost as an afterthought she said, "I'm here in town, at a friend's — 643-7298."

Reggie anxiously punched in the numbers. When Kathy answered he said, "Kathy? Is everything OK?"

"Thank God," said Kathy; "I was afraid you weren't going to call."

"What are you doing here? Are your parents all right?" Reggie suddenly remembered that Kathy had grown up near Capital City.

"What? Oh — they're fine," Kathy said, remembering the excuse she had given Arlene. "Reggie, I need to see you. Can I come over?" When Reggie paused she added, plaintively, "Please?"

"Of course," he said. "I guess that would be all right." Reggie paused. "Should we meet in the lobby?"

"I'll come to your room," Kathy said. "I'm about ten minutes away."

When Kathy arrived, she was out of breath, as if she had been running. When Reggie closed the door she embraced him, trembling. "Oh, Reggie," she said. "I really needed to see you." She began to cry.

"What's wrong?" Reggie was truly alarmed now.

Kathy sat in one of the two side chairs beside the room's small table, composing herself. At the last minute she decided not to tell Reggie about the letter she had left for Rob, the letter telling him she wanted a divorce. "I just couldn't face a week without seeing you," she finally said.

Flattered, unsure what was happening, Reggie sat down in the other chair. Flooded with a mixture of feelings, he said nothing.

"Reggie, can I stay here tonight?" Seeing him look at the bed Kathy laughed. "There are two beds, Reggie. I just don't want to be alone tonight."

"What about your friend?"

"She's not even home. She just left a key for me under a plant." Kathy smiled. "Actually, she doesn't spend much time there anymore. She's usually at her boyfriend's."

When Reggie still said nothing, looking more and more anxious, Kathy stood. "All right. I can see this bothers you. I'll go back to the apartment."

"No!" Reggie realized his voice was sharp. "Of course, you can stay. I want you to stay."

They talked until 1:30, until Reggie was falling asleep. As Kathy went into the bathroom, Reggie undressed and got into bed. A few minutes later Kathy came out of the bathroom, still wearing her clothes, and crawled into the other bed.

Reggie fell asleep, later awakening with a start. The bedside clock said that it was 3:15. He got up and went to the bathroom. On the way back, he impulsively climbed into Kathy's bed. After a minute he moved next to her and put his arm around her. When she did not move he cupped her breast in his hand.

She was not asleep. "Reggie, don't. Please. I don't want to spoil it with sex."

After another minute he released her breast, and moved to get out of the bed. "No," she said. "Don't go. Just stay here next to me."

She pulled his arm back around her, and after a few more minutes they both fell back asleep.

When Reggie awoke sunlight was streaming through the opening between the window's curtains. As he realized where he was and who he was with he turned to look at Kathy, who was lying on her side watching him. He looked at the clock. "Damn! I was supposed to meet Andy for breakfast five minutes ago!" It was the first time she had heard him swear.

Reggie rushed into the bathroom. When he came out, Kathy was sitting on one of the chairs. "Go ahead and get ready," she said; "I'll use the bathroom after you leave."

"What are you going to do today? Will I see you tonight?"

"I'm going by my parents' house," she said. "To make the trip legitimate. Then I'm going home." When Reggie looked disappointed she added, "I'm not sure I can remain chaste another night." She smiled. After a moment Reggie also smiled.

Realizing he was standing before her in his underwear, Reggie moved to pull on the slacks he had thrown over the other chair when he undressed for bed. He pulled a white knit shirt from his suitcase and over his head, self-consciously tucking it into his pants. When the telephone rang they, both jumped.

"Damn!" He looked at Kathy. "I was supposed to call Lillian." Kathy grimaced and moved toward the bathroom. But it was Andy, wondering if Reggie had forgotten their date. Reggie told him he was on his way.

As Reggie grabbed his wallet, loose change, and room key, Kathy waited for him near the door. "Thanks for letting me stay," she said. "I can't tell you how important it was to have you be there for me." She reached her arms around him, pulled him close, and kissed him hard on the mouth.

"I'll see you at church Sunday," Reggie said, opening the door. "It was really good to see you — to be with you." He felt awkward, unable to say what he wanted. As he started down the hall toward the elevator she stood in the doorway, watching.

Reggie thought he heard her say, "I love you, Reggie," but he was afraid to look back.

*

Rob Leighter was quite drunk when he got home Tuesday evening, and he stumbled to bed without seeing Kathy's letter. When the alarm woke him the next morning and he realized that Kathy was not there, he found and read the letter. Then he telephoned work to say he would not be in, that he "had the flu." After a few minutes of agitated pacing, he placed a call to Kathy's parents.

"Oh, Rob," said Janet Leighter, Kathy's mother. "Kathy's not here yet. I think she stayed with a friend in the city last night."

"Thanks, Janet," Rob said. "Could you have Kathy call me when she gets in? I'll be at home."

"Is everything all right?" Janet wondered if Rob had again lost his job.

"Yeah, things are OK," he replied. "I think I'm coming down with the flu. I'm going to stay home today."

"Oh. Well, take care of yourself, dear. I'll have Kathy call."

Rob made some coffee to try to clear his head, then read the letter again. He looked at the clock, then looked up the telephone number for First Community Church. When the secretary, Arlene, told him that Pastor Arnold was in Capital City for a few days he slammed down the phone. Enraged, he charged around the apartment, going nowhere, then slumped into a chair.

He was still sitting there when the telephone rang.

"I suppose you read the letter." Kathy had not even said hello.

"What the hell do you think you're doing? Where were you last night? And don't give me any crap about being at your parents!"

"I was at Jeannie's, Rob. Don't yell at me! We can talk when I get back."

"And when the hell will that be?"

"I'll be back late this evening."

"Sure. I suppose you want to spend a little more time with that preacher."

Kathy blanched. "What are you talking about?"

"Don't shit me, Kath. I know what's been going on." He slammed down the phone again.

Kathy looked at her mother. "I'm sorry, Mom. I have to get back right away."

"But you just got here. Your Dad's not even back from the doctor's yet. Is everything all right?"

"Yes. No. I'll call you as soon as I can. I promise I'll be back for a real visit soon." Kathy picked up her purse and ran to the door.

"Kathy! Wait!" Then, as Kathy rushed into her car, "Be careful!"

By the time Kathy got home she was resolved. When Rob approached her angrily she stopped him. "Just listen to me! Rob, please hear me out!"

Rob slumped onto the couch.

"Rob, our marriage has been in the toilet for years! I don't know if it could possibly be saved. I don't know if you can ever stop drinking. I don't know if you can ever hold a job more than three months." She took in a breath and then added, "And I don't know if I can ever forgive you for what you did to me that night." It was the first time the rape had ever been mentioned between them.

Rob started to say something, to defend himself; but in the end, he only slumped further into the couch, defeated.

"OK. I admit I've been spending a lot of time with Pastor . . . with Reggie Arnold. He, at least, appreciates me, listens to me. But nothing has ever happened between us. You've got to believe that." She decided to omit any reference to last night and, to her relief, Rob did not ask.

"But things are getting out of hand. So, here's what I've decided to do." She took a deep breath. "I'm moving back to Capital City. I'm pretty sure I can get a transfer back to the main office there. Even if I can't, I'm going. Right away. As soon as possible."

She looked at Rob. He sat slumped on the couch.

Finally, she softened. "Look, Rob. I don't know if our marriage can be saved or not. I really don't think it can. For sure, I know it can't be saved unless you stop drinking, unless you make a lot of changes." A long pause, then, "but if you want to come with me, you can."

"What about my job?"

Kathy looked at him, astounded. "Jesus, Rob! You've gotten and lost more jobs than an employment office! You can damn well get another job in Capital City!"

Rob burst into tears. Through trembling lips, he mumbled, "Maybe we can get counseling."

Kathy stared. "How many times have I asked you. . ." she began, before deciding to let the matter drop.

That afternoon Kathy called her supervisor. "Virginia, things are worse than I thought when we talked yesterday. I have to move back to Capital City right away." She paused, then offered the best reason she had been able to come up with: "Mother's failing, and my Dad's not doing well at all. Can you check to see if that opening in the Capital City office is still available?"

Thirty minutes later Virginia Allen called back. "It's been filled, Kathy." Kathy sagged. "But there's a management position opening up. When Central Office heard you wanted to come back they wanted you there yesterday!" Kathy sat, stunned, and began to cry softly.

"I'll start the paperwork today," Virginia said. "If I let you go immediately will you remember me when you become an Assistant Director?"

"Virginia, you've just saved my life! I'll never forget this."

When Kathy left for her office to see Virginia and to clean out her desk Rob dug out the First Church telephone directory. He had a few calls to make himself. The first person he dialed was Lillian Arnold.

That night, after everyone had left, Kathy slipped her letter of resignation under the church office door. When Arlene read the letter, in which Kathy listed as reasons her mother's health and that her husband had been transferred to Capital City, she looked at Reggie Arnold's closed office door.

"This one is going to shake the pillars," she thought. Arlene had long suspected that Reggie and Kathy discussed more than Sunday morning music.

*

Reggie Arnold was horrified when he stopped by the church on the way home and learned that Kathy had resigned, and that rumors of his affair with her were racing through the congregation. When he arrived home, it was apparent that Lil also knew.

He denied everything, of course. Yes, he had spent time with her over the past few weeks; she was very troubled about her marriage. But they had never been involved. Still, perhaps it was best she was gone.

Lillian was not persuaded, but decided not to tell Reggie everything she knew — that she had talked to Rob, that she and Arlene had talked, that she had found the restaurant credit card charges. She was, as always, a very practical woman.

She did observe Reggie become morose, spending a lot of time alone. Twice she saw him crying, but decided to say nothing.

At church, Reggie was just "going through the motions," unsure how to stem the tide of rumors. He became increasingly sure, however, that he could not continue as pastor; so, when the chairman of the denomination's regional ministerial conference called he was ready. He submitted his resignation to the First Church Board on December third, effective December 31st. When, two months later, a seldom-seen former parishioner offered him a job selling insurance, he accepted it. Reggie knew he was unfit for pastoral work; and Lillian had too good a job for them to consider leaving the area.

In time, of course, things died down, as things usually do. The rumors subsided, and since neither Reggie nor Lil were around First Church, members of the congregation began to worry about other things. Reggie began to resolve his feelings about Kathy, moving through anguish to anger, and then just sadness. He and

Lillian forged a sometimes strained, but workable, relationship. Occasionally, after particularly good days, they even made love.

Reggie was still depressed, of course, but he began to think of that as having more to do with his job than with Kathy or his marriage. He had not been particularly successful in insurance, and if it were not for his guaranteed draw he and Lillian would have trouble making it financially. Still, he (and they) persevered, not being sure what else to do.

*

It was two years later, when Reggie was in Capital City to attend a training session at the State Insurance Commission, that he saw Kathy. She was coming out of a restaurant near the state office building with two other women; and when she saw Reggie standing across the street watching her she sent the women on and crossed over to him.

"It's been a long time."

Reggie, not knowing what to say or do, just stared.

"Look," said Kathy. "I'm going to take the afternoon off. Let's get some coffee."

When Reggie started to protest she touched his lip with her finger, stopping him. Reaching into her purse, she extracted a cell phone and called her office. Reggie decided to ditch the rest of the training session. He hadn't understood much of it anyway, and had come to realize he would never be able to make a career in insurance.

They spent the afternoon talking. Kathy apologized for running away, but Reggie had come to understand that she had done what had to be done. She was doing well, had gotten a promotion, and liked her new job very much. She and Rob had tried for a while, although they never got into counseling. Finally, when Rob resumed drinking, they had divorced.

"I'm sorry, Kathy. I feel like I'm responsible."

"Don't. My marriage was doomed from the beginning. If anything, you helped to prolong it."

Reggie was doubtful, but let it pass. He told Kathy what had happened at the church, what he was doing now. Surprisingly, Kathy seemed to already know; apparently, she had kept up through old work associates in Spring City. She asked how Lillian was, hoped she was doing well.

"We're doing as well as can be expected, considering." Reggie did not feel comfortable talking about his marriage. "I really don't like selling insurance, though. I envy you your good job."

Kathy smiled, reached out and touched his hand. "You know, I didn't have a chance to tell you why I was so upset the night we were together here."

Reggie looked at her, surprised that she brought it up.

"I had left Rob a letter telling him I wanted a divorce."

Reggie looked at her, astounded. "You didn't think . . ."

"No, of course not. I knew you would never leave Lillian. I wouldn't have wanted you if you could have. That's why I knew I had to leave."

Tears appeared in Reggie's eyes, and Kathy reached across the table for his hand. "Reggie Arnold, you were the best thing that had ever come into my life. Maybe the best thing that ever will. But your life is with Lillian and your girls. I always knew that." And then, after a minute, she added, "And don't you dare worry about me! I'm doing very well! Even with losing you I'm happier than I've ever been."

They continued to talk throughout the afternoon, walking around a downtown park. Their conversation seemed natural, comfortable, as if they had just parted a day or two before. When

Kathy walked Reggie back to his car she reached again for his hand, then pulled him close. Kissing him lightly on the lips, she pulled away and smiled. "Thank you, Reggie Arnold. I don't think you realize it, but you probably saved my life."

Then she turned and walked away.

Reggie told Lilly about seeing Kathy, and about skipping the training, the next evening, when they were finally alone. She looked at him, warily.

"How is she?"

"She seems to be doing great. She's gotten a promotion, is apparently making good money. She and Rob are divorced."

Lilly looked at him, sharply. Something seemed different about Reggie.

Reggie read her glance, understanding. "Lil, you really don't need to worry about Kathy. You're stuck with me — I'm not going anywhere."

He paused, uncertain how to broach the other subject. Finally, he said, "But I am going to quit my job. I know I'm not cut out for insurance. I'm surprised I haven't been fired by now."

Lil laughed. "If you keep ditching training meetings I'm sure you will be."

"I can find another job, Lil. If not, I can go back to school." It was the most optimistic thing he had said in the last two years.

Lilly looked at Reggie, then stood to go into the kitchen. "I'm sure you can," she finally said. "We'll work it out."

It took Reggie two more days to tell Lilly the other thing that was on his mind, the other thing that Kathy had said to him just before they parted.

He tried to sound casual, off-handed. "You know, Kathy Leighter said something interesting when we talked the other day." Lillian stopped what she was doing, looking back to hear what Reggie was about to say.

Reggie omitted the way Kathy had said it, that she had whispered it into his ear as they kissed goodbye. "She said she thought . . ." He paused, trying to compose himself. What Kathy had actually said was, "Listen to me, Reggie Arnold. This is what I want you to do." "She said she thought I should go back into church work. She said she thought I was a very good pastor."

Lillian paused, then walked into the kitchen. "She's right," she said. "You were — are — the best pastor I've ever known."

True Stories

Jean's Song[*]

1) Memory's End

*D*riving through pouring rain deep into the night the man
grew quiet, so that his wife eventually fell asleep. He dreaded
what lay ahead, realized a week earlier when he had called
his mother on Saturday and learned that she was "getting ready for
church." He had tried to convince her that it was Saturday afternoon,
not Sunday morning, but she could not understand.

A friend in his mother's town confirmed her confusion: she had
shown up for church at 7 AM Sunday, ringing the Pastor's doorbell
when the church door was locked; had not been there when church did
begin at 10:45; had been there again at 7 AM Monday. The man had,
therefore, already made arrangements for his mother's admission to a
nearby Southwest Missouri hospital geriatric program.

Driving through the rain, locked into himself, he knew that his
mother would never return home. Each mile took them closer to the
emotional minefield ahead.

------

[*]A version of this story first appeared in the July 26, 2000 edition
of the *St. Louis Post-Dispatch,* under the headline *"Alzheimer's takes
mother and son on a painful, bewildering journey."*

The first clue, unrecognized at the time, was in late August, in response to a casual question about what she had eaten for lunch. The predictable menu, from her highly regimented and restricted food list, included grapes. Mother had long since excluded all fruit, except bananas, from her diet.

"At least she's eating a little better," I suggested wistfully to my wife, Marilyn. "Or maybe she's forgotten that she stopped eating fruit."

The week before Halloween Mother mentioned that she had, as usual, gone to the bank for ten dollars' worth of quarters to give to trick-or-treaters (a futile annual tradition because she would then turn off her lights and sit in the dark, so no one would think she was home). She also mentioned buying a bag of "little things wrapped up to give out."

It turned out she was describing Halloween-sized chocolate bars. A week later she mentioned eating "one or two," a surprising and disturbing development, considering that she had not eaten candy for years, convinced that that was the reason she was "the only one in the family who had never gotten diabetes." By the week before our planned December visit it became apparent that candy was all she was eating.

Returning to the house after leaving Mother at the hospital we found two dozen packages of various kinds of candy, arrayed on the unused north bedroom bed. There were also four dozen bottles of extra-strength acetaminophen, at least twelve opened and partially used, 24 bottles of Aleve, and assorted other pain medications.

It was hardly surprising that she was unable to function. The unanswerable question was which came first: the dementia, or the diet and drug abuse? Would things have been different if I had intervened and forced an earlier move?

Driving into Golden City on the cold, clearing Friday morning we stopped at the library. Carol, the librarian, was a friend of Mother's and our most reliable resource during the months Mother's dementia was developing. The word of our coming was out: a list of friends and neighbors wanted to see us.

The Postmaster said Mother had been "mailing" letters with canceled stamps and Easter Seals. The owner of the local grocery (largely kept in business with Mother's compulsive purchases) expressed his concern. Neighbors, noting her repetitive daily walks to and from home to the post office or the bank or the grocery were concerned she would fall when the weather worsened.

Ostensibly, our visit was to take Mother for her quarterly doctor's visit. I could not tell her, driving the 35 miles to the doctor's office, that she would not be going home. How do you tell someone, however confused, that life as they have known it is over? And how, especially, do you say that in the context of more than sixty years of unaddressed and unresolved mutual disappointments?

Waiting at the hospital Mother fixed me with her fiercest glare. "Let's just forget this," she said, as assertively as she could muster, "and go home."

"We can't do that, Mom," I replied. What else was there to say?

After her admission we talked with the social worker before going back into the Unit say goodbye to Mother. It was dinner and she was sitting before a plate of partially-eaten roast beef, mashed potatoes and green beans, foods she had refused to eat for years. As we approached she looked up, then bit off a huge piece of dinner roll.

On the way out of the hospital the man stopped at a rest room. Men his age seldom pass bathrooms before long drives. And empty bathrooms are good places for men his age to cry.

71

2) The Nursing Home

*This is the way the man imagined that the old woman's story —
repeated over and over again — about how she had "walked all the
way home" was created:*

*She had been awakened at 5:30 AM by hospital staff for the trip to
St. Louis. She was dressed, fed breakfast, and bundled into the hospital's
van; and before fully awake she was watching interstate scenery flow
past the van's side window.*

*Clarity and confusion must have moved hand-in-hand through
her awareness. Brief moments of realization that she was indeed being
moved, against her will and by her son, to a "home" in St. Louis would
have alternated with long periods of confusion, her mind wandering
through stupor to memory to fantasy. Through it all she would only
know that she wanted to go home, would go home as soon as she could.*

*Her mind would have drifted to the roadside and the trees and the
road signs sliding past, drifted outside the van to the roadside itself,
coalesced around the image of walking, walking home, no matter how
far or how impossible. Cars and trucks would roar pass, but let them:
she would just step aside and keep walking. Soon, eventually, some day
she would see familiar sights, recognize where she was, find herself back
in Golden City.*

*She would do what she had always said she would do, had always
known she would do: she would run away. Meanwhile, the man
imagined, she drifted along with the van, rolling toward St. Louis.*

It is hard to imagine being *ready* to move a parent into a nursing
home: there are too many considerations, too many issues, too many
emotions to have possibly done all the ground-work needed for such
a decision. Nursing home placements involve failure – failure of the
parent to function adequately, failure of the child to assist, failure
to care, failure to protect. And there are losses, too many losses,

whether the parent was good and loving or angry and abusive: the loss of vitality and function by the aging parent, the loss of nurture and support that once existed or that was always wanted even if it never existed, even the realization that similar losses lie in one's own future.

In addition, there are the stories, horror stories, of ill-treatment, neglect, even abuse. The realization that workers in residential care, providing care for aging, cantankerous, senile (and, too often, cast aside) old people are among the least valued workers in our society, poorly paid and overworked and, therefore, over-stressed. The recognition that we are entrusting our parents, the very persons who raised *us*, to care-takers to whom we would never entrust our children.

And there is never enough time to make a decision. How can one compare and contrast fifty or sixty different nursing homes, keep relevant factors straight, make a reasoned choice? Where does one begin? How can you balance cleanliness, services, programming, or food service against staff turnover, odor, or administrative neglect? How can one *ever know?*

We were lucky, I suppose: Marilyn has worked in home-based and hospice health care for twenty years, has been in dozens of nursing homes, and knows nurses and social workers that have been in others. I had clients who knew the ins and outs, hidden secrets, key questions. We were able to weed the choices down to six or seven, to visit most of those, to secure validation for our decision, and to find a bed within a week.

Mother arrived on the Tuesday before Christmas, driven the 270 miles across the state by the hospital's geriatric evaluation unit staff. She seemed to understand what was happening, but quickly deteriorated into confusion, wanting to go home, resume her life. At times she seemed to think she was "working," a reflection, we assumed, of her prior career as an LPN. And each time we saw her she would repeat the same "story:" about walking home, just "walking and walking alongside the road, stepping into the ditch when a car would come by," until finally she began to recognize where she was.

On the Friday before Christmas Eve we found her deathly ill, suffering from a 24-hour virus raging through the nursing home. Holding her hand, watching her be sick in the bathroom, I was terrified: my worst fear had always been that I would move her, and she would immediately die. By Christmas Day she was better, but we were not, spending Christmas night alternating in the bathroom. It was, I mumbled, kneeling over the commode, "Mother's curse."

So, it was not difficult for the man to imagine her sitting at a table, watching as people came and went, one after another pushing the particular button and waiting for the doors to open that would take them away.

And one day, a week or so after arriving, she packed some socks and underwear in a bag, included a calendar about Jesus' "footprints in the sand," and waited for the nurses to leave the station in front of the elevators. Hurrying over, she pushed the button, and when the doors opened slipped inside.

3) Going Home

She walked into the suburban police station about 4 PM on a Sunday afternoon in February, lost, confused, and frightened. She wore two sweaters but no coat and no hat. When the officers asked her where she lived she said, "Golden City." When they asked if she had been in a nursing home she said, "Yes, I think so." They called the closest home, nearly two miles away, verified that she was a resident, and drove her back.

When her son talked with her later that evening she was still confused, not remembering at first, then gradually supplied a few details. She had been "going home," but nothing was familiar; the cars went by "very fast," and she was "scared." Her son deduced that she had taken advantage of Sunday afternoon visiting hour's confusion to open an alarmed fire door and go down five flights of stairs.

It was not her first trip off the floor, of course, and it would not be her last.

Driving to Golden City on a clear, crisp Thursday evening in January Marilyn commented that it was the first trip in several months that not been marred by heavy rain. It was also the first time we were not going to see Mother, who we had hospitalized a month earlier and who was now in a St. Louis nursing home. We were going to Golden City to begin clearing out Mother's home.

There is something invasive about cleaning out someone's home, exposing all those real-life secrets each of us withhold from all but our closest living companions: the kind of toilet paper we buy, the condition of our underwear, what we keep in back-room drawers. But these are also the data from which one might infer inner secrets: what has been going on in our heart of hearts and mind of minds.

Mother had been hoarding, a behavior we had observed for years. What we did not know was the extent, the strangeness, of the hoarding: drawers of plastic room deodorant cones; a kitchen drawer filled with more than a hundred scotch-tape dispensers, many used up but put back in the drawer; box after box of Bran Chex, many carefully removed from the store carton and re-stored in round empty oatmeal boxes; bottles and bottles of lotion, boxes and boxes of tissues, and packages and packages of Woolite. But, surprisingly, no stock of toilet paper.

As we filled trash bag after trash bag Marilyn said, "When we get home we're throwing all our stuff out. I'm not going to have our kids talk about us the way we're talking about your mother!" (But we didn't, of course; one of the reasons we store up strange things is we don't think they are strange; and besides, who has time to clean out old drawers?)

And, gradually, as is so often the case, the obvious began to become clear: how much Mother had been holding herself together with ritual and routine. She went to the store over and over each day because that was a learned behavior that *kept her on track*, which she could remember and repeat. She bought things when she got there, of course, the same things she always bought, not because she needed them but because she *remembered* them.

Which is why she keeps trying to leave the nursing home, of course: she has used "going" as the way to remember, to keep on track, to cope with the anxiety and fear of losing her mind, for years. Her repeated efforts to leave, to open the alarmed doors, are less about "escaping" than they are about "remembering." The problem is that she is remembering rituals from another time and another place, rituals that no longer apply and no longer work.

At the suggestion of the home's Director of Nursing we have moved Mother to another unit, on the ground floor. Also locked, it is a special needs unit, with fewer residents, so she should get more attention. And because it is not primarily for Alzheimer's residents she should be able to keep personal items, such as pictures, on her dresser.

Hopefully, that will help her begin to identify her room as "home," a place of some safety. We are also beginning to take her out, to our home, perhaps to places she might enjoy in St. Louis like parks or the zoo.

Of course, she still tries to leave every day. It is, at this point in her life, who she is, what she does.

When the old woman tells her son now about the time she tried to walk "all the way home," and how the cars "went by fast," and how she "stepped aside into the ditch and then back onto the street," he knows that it is not all fantasy.

Somehow, in her confusion, she has made some part of fantasy into reality.

4) The Face of Alzheimer's

So, this is the face of Alzheimer's: an old woman, sitting slumped, head bowed, in the oversized chair.

She was asleep, indistinguishable in manner from the many other ancients scattered about in wheel chairs or other furniture. He recognized her because she wore on her head the knit cap, the one she had knitted herself in a younger and more capable day. She also wore white hospital pants, black shoes he knew to be someone else's, and a beautiful knit sweater, another of her creations. Over the sweater lay a heavy cloth bib.

When he awoke her she was confused, lethargic, surprised — as always, despite his twice-weekly visits — to see him. "I'm so glad to see you," she mumbled. "You'll never know how long I've wanted to see you."

She had difficulty getting out of the chair, and walked with him to her room with the shuffling gait of the institutionalized.

My wife read over the text of a brief bio I had written for the two of us in response to a request from our church's newsletter editor. I had mentioned how and when we had met, and described our life together: our family moves, our two careers, and our children.

"You should say something about our mothers," she said.

I added a paragraph mentioning that both of our mothers are in nursing homes, Marilyn's mother with "end-stage Alzheimer's," and mine with what "appears to be Alzheimer's."

"Appears," she asked? "I don't understand why you are so uncomfortable with saying that your mother has Alzheimer's. She's been diagnosed four times."

I began to respond defensively, to say, "Only twice!" Then, in true male fashion, I ended up saying nothing. But I have reflected on her charge, and I think I am beginning to understand some of my discomfort with Alzheimer's: it scares the hell out of me.

Alzheimer's, if anything, is about loss. But not *just* loss — it is loss in the midst of *presence*. Nothing seems more terrifying than not being here even though one — one's body — still *is* here. Nothing, that is, except that period of the progression of the disease when one is aware, in some disintegrating fashion, of one's growing lack of awareness.

And then, inexplicably, embarrassingly, there is for me something of a *moral* quality to Alzheimer's — a sense of *badness,* as if someone must have done something terribly wrong to achieve this state. It is irrational, I know, and I have been struggling to understand and move beyond this limiting sense.

Embarrassing, but perhaps not so inexplicable. Beyond the inevitable and perhaps universal sense of loss, beyond the inevitable and perhaps universal fears of inheritance, there lies, for me, the reality of what I now understand to have been an *unholy contract*: my implicit understanding that it was *my* job to make *her* life — miserable though it may have been at times — worthwhile. *I* was to be her salvation, her protector from the fearfulness – greatly exaggerated – we complicity agreed my step-father represented.

I could not do that, of course. I could not protect her, not even from whatever *actual* danger my step-father in fact presented. I could never "make her happy."

Of course, I know who failed. *I* failed.

This, then, is the face of Alzheimer's: an old woman's face when she realizes the truth.

The man and his wife had taken her from the nursing home for the first time, for a visit to their home, a home she had never seen. They had shown her the house, had lunched, and talked. And although much of her conversation was confused, mixing fantasy with remembrance, she had brightened throughout the afternoon.

Toward the end of the afternoon the woman had begun to talk of going home, asking over and over if her son would take her there so she could "get her checkbook" and go to the bank for some money: "Sixty dollars, one twenty, two tens, two fives, and ten ones." Patiently, repeatedly, he had told her they could not, that it was too far, that she could not stay alone there anymore.

Finally, they returned to the nursing home. They drove up and entered the building, walked down the long halls to the "special needs unit," removed her coat and visited her room. When they were preparing to leave she said to him, "So you're going to leave me here? How long will I have to stay?"

He could not tell her the truth: that she would be there forever. He mumbled something about her needing to stay here "for now," and backed away. But he watched as his wife approached her to say goodbye.

And as the two women embraced he saw his mother's tears.

Making Something Happen:
The Hugs and Kisses Project

F riday dawned cold and blustery as the dented van nosed into a parking space across Water Street from the Maritime Building. An icy wind blew across southern Manhattan, chilling the half-dozen individuals donning matching caps and pulling jacket-collars up. It was four days before Christmas, and less than four months after Lower Manhattan had been decimated by the destruction of the World Trade Center.

The group's destination was Battery Park, a 21-acre expanse jutting into Upper New York Bay on the island's southwestern tip and, at State Street, the site of the terminus of the Staten Island Ferry. The gray sky was beginning to lighten as group members, each wearing "XOXO" on their caps, began pulling cards from canvas mail bags and offering them to men and women disembarking from the ferry.

Many of the commuters, hurrying north toward the remaining office buildings, ignored the cards with averted eyes. Others – accustomed, perhaps to taking and then disposing of tracts and other such offerings – took one and hurried on. Occasionally someone would slow, reading what they had been given, and glance back. One or two, with tears in their eyes, turned back.

X O X O

Deb Lavender was getting ready to start her day on the Tuesday that was September 11, 2001 — drinking a cup of tea, watching a

81

pair of wrens fight over birdseed in her backyard feeder, and running a comb through her reddish-blond hair while telephoning a friend in California — when something on the television she had been ignoring caught her ear. She glanced up in time to see the second of two airplanes crash into the World Trade Center buildings.

Lavender, a trim 45-year-old physical therapist living in suburban St. Louis, Missouri, was as stunned as every other American on that fateful day. She knew New York, having grown up in nearby Connecticut. She had been to Manhattan, had admired the skyline dominated by the Trade Center towers. Furthermore, her entire family – her mother, older sister Elise, and younger siblings Alan, Wayne and Diane – all lived in the New York metropolitan area.

Lavender watched, transfixed, for a few moments; and then, realizing she was going to be late for work, ran to her car. As she drove, fumbling for information on her car's radio dial, she heard that one of the World Trade towers had fallen. Suddenly, Lavender's concerns became personal: Elise, she realized, traveled to work every day by a subway train that passed directly *under* the World Trade Center.

Keeping track of family members, worrying about their welfare, was Lavender's family role, despite – or perhaps because of – her living so far away. Driving with one hand, she punched numbers into her cell phone. Both Elise's work number and her mother's home number were busy. Finally, she reached Alan.

"Alan," she yelled when he answered. "Have you heard from Elise? I heard that the tower fell!"

"Both towers, Deb," Alan replied. "Thousands trapped." It had not occurred to Alan to worry about his sister.

"I can't reach her, Alan. Will you try? Let me know if you hear anything."

Pulling into her office parking lot Lavender tried one more number: Elise's home. Maybe Elise had been sick this morning; or had been late leaving for work and, hearing about the attack, had decided to stay home. Or, maybe, Elise's husband Craig, a Methodist minister, had left for the church a little later than usual. Not really expecting an answer, she was surprised to hear her mother's voice. Of course — today was one of the two Tuesdays each month when Mom went to Elise's house to clean.

Janet Schnitzher, who had had the television on when the attack began, had been watching the developments unfold. But it had not occurred to her to worry about her daughter either. She tried to console Lavender. "I'm sure Elise is OK, Deb," she said. "But you can call her. I have her new cell phone number."

Lavender dialed the number while still in the parking lot. Cell phones in New York City were not working.

X O X O

It was noon before the call came telling Lavender that Elise was safe, and several more hours before the sisters were able to talk. Elise had left home early for work, passing beneath the Trade Towers about 8:00 AM, and had been in her office, less than a half-mile to the west, when the first tower was hit. Hearing the explosion, she had felt the shock wave a moment later.

Standing at the office's conference room window Elise watched in horror as another airplane plowed into the second tower. She and her co-workers quickly concluded that they needed to get out of their building.

Knowing she needed to leave the area, but unsure where to go, Elise had boarded the subway and crossed under the Hudson River into Manhattan, heading uptown. When the first tower fell she and the other riders could feel the shock wave, as powerful as an earthquake. The train was halted, and Elise ran up the subway steps. Immediately assaulted by clouds of dust and shrieking sirens, Elise looked south, watching in horror as the second tower collapsed, its antenna seeming to fall at her feet. Shaken and terrified, she joined hundreds of dazed individuals hurrying north.

Elise headed toward Grand Central Station, only to find it closed. She walked a few blocks to Christ Church, a United Methodist Church, and entered the sanctuary to try to pull herself together. Alternately crying and praying, she waited for the noon service promised on the outside message board.

When she realized there would be no service Elise returned to Grand Central, and found it briefly open. Boarding a train for home, she checked her cell phone and realized that she had a signal.

At 1:00 PM New York time Elise was finally able to let her family know she was safe.

X O X O

It is hard to know what, finally, prompted Deb Lavender to action. She shared with most Americans an immediate desire to do something, *anything*, in response to the horrifying, infuriating, irrational attack. Her more personal connection, with family intimately affected, may have added motivation. And, as she would certainly tell you herself, she is a woman more inclined toward action than reflection.

In the end, however, most Americans, even those with personal connections, could find nothing to do after the terrorist attacks, and finally returned helplessly to their pre-September 11th lives. So, it may be that it was Lavender's involvement in Landmark Education that, in the end, provided the mandate, structure and support she needed.

Developed by Werner Erhard, the founder of "EST" (Erhard Seminar Training) in 1971, Landmark is dedicated to the study of "what it means to be human." Lavender began taking Landmark courses and seminars in 1996, finally becoming a course supervisor. The last weekend in September 2001, Lavender had driven to

Chicago for a Landmark Education "classroom," a weekend training seminar for course supervisors.

The seminar leader was Beth Jones, a financial broker from New York. Jones, whose office was in a building on Wall Street a short distance from the towers, began the weekend by describing her experiences on the day of the attacks. Having decided to evacuate her office personnel after the towers were hit, Jones had led her staff down the stairs to the street just as the first tower fell. Confronted with billowing smoke, dust and debris, and following the advice of nearby emergency personnel, she was forced to lead her employees back into the very building she had just deemed unsafe.

It was a powerful story, deeply moving. Caught up in Beth Jones' story and still reacting to the emotions of the past two weeks, Lavender's desire to act fermented. She wanted, needed, to do something.

Shortly after returning home Lavender received an e-mail from a friend who lived in New York. Nancy Gorman, her husband, and most of her friends had lost family members or friends in the towers. The last sentence of her e-mail, "We just stay angry, so we can cope," hit Lavender like a sledge hammer. How terrible to have to live with such anger, however understandable it might be. She could not get her friend's words out of her head; and every time they returned, she found herself in tears.

A week later, on October 16th, Lavender was preparing to be a coach for a Landmark "Self Expression and Leadership Program" course. One aspect of SELP courses is that students are required to develop and complete community service projects. Lavender's role, as a coach, involved supporting three or four students in their projects, but she would also be required to complete a project of her own.

As Lavender talked with Tommie Wehrle, the course instructor, the subject of the types of projects they might anticipate after the September 11th attack came up. Suddenly, in the inexplicable way that intuition works, like a lock's tumblers falling one by one, the pieces fell into place. New Yorkers had been devastated, left angry and alone. St. Louisans, like everybody else, wanted to reach out, connect, comfort. She would do something for both: she would collect holiday cards from people in St. Louis and deliver them to people in New York.

She even had the perfect name for her idea: "The Hugs & Kisses Project."

X O X O

Although intended to impact on community needs, SELP projects, like all Landmark experiences, are primarily about self-development. There was learning to be done, even in an unsuccessful project.

Hugs & Kisses was not Lavender's first SELP project. The first time she took the course her project idea was to create housing in a largely segregated and impoverished "near north side" neighborhood of St. Louis, to "transform a neighborhood." But it was much too big a project to be achievable by someone without connections or resources and, in the end, she did little or nothing on it.

That does not mean, however, that the effort was entirely without value. After processing the difficulties she had encountered Lavender concluded that her first problem had been that she did not think that she was "good enough" to accomplish an idea. What she learned, in addition to practical lessons about size and resource needs, was that she could talk herself out of an idea before she ever got started.

X O X O

"It takes a village," Hillary Clinton has suggested, "to raise a child." It also takes a village to pull off a good idea.

Of course, you have to get the village involved.

86

One of the first persons Lavender told about her project idea, in late October, was Nancy Quigle, a long-time friend. Quigle was a 50-something former city manager and occasional real estate agent who was between jobs. Lavender and Quigle would touch base every month or so; and it was in one of these telephone calls that Lavender outlined her idea. "Before I had finished telling her the plan," Lavender later said, "Nancy asked if she could help."

Hugs & Kisses was clearly Lavender's project, but Quigle was intimately involved in almost every step. One of the first things they did was derive a project logo. The name, "Hugs & Kisses," had been suggested in the SELP meeting in which the idea arose. Even more ingenious, perhaps, was the addition of "XOXO" as a project logo.

Logos, like names, are more than labels: they become *representations* of the things they designate. They need to be eye-catching, easily remembered, and communicate something essential about the project. Visual, universally understood, and easily produced graphically, XOXO quickly became the symbolic representation of the Hugs & Kisses Project, easily displayed on caps and other project materials.

On October 21st Lavender represented her employer at the St. Louis Marathon, providing whatever services runners might need. During the course of the morning she spotted Randi Naughton, a sports reporter for KTVI, the St. Louis' Fox TV outlet. Naughton was wearing a New York Fire Department cap and reporting on the children's one-mile run.

Lavender struck up a conversation with Naughton, who commented that she had been in New York, visiting "ground zero," the previous week. Lavender outlined her idea and asked if "Fox 2 News" would be interested in covering the story.

"I think we would," Naughton said, giving Deb her card. "Keep us informed."

Also covering the marathon was Kim Lee, an intern photographer for the *St. Louis Post-Dispatch,* who also expressed interest in the story and promised to talk with an editor when he got back to the newspaper's office.

Lavender and Quigle began to piece together a project outline, identifying key elements: the need for publicity, for funding, and for such tactical support as collection sites and transportation to New York. Quigle took responsibility for installing a telephone line dedicated to the project and began looking for collection sites and media support.

Lavender began telling regular contacts about her idea. Several physicians donated money, enough to cover the telephone line and more. Tim Williams, a vice-president of Crown Linen, a company that launders towels and linens for medical facilities, agreed to provide laundry bags to carry cards to New York.

"How many bags do you think you'll need?" he asked, when Lavender called him.

Lavender had not thought about numbers. "Do you think we could get a hundred?"

There was a moment of silence on the other end of the line. Williams had probably been thinking in terms of six or eight bags. Then, without further comment, he agreed. "A hundred bags it is."

Perhaps most significant (and essential) was the support offered by ProRehab, Lavender's employer. Although the Hugs & Kisses phone line was handled by Nancy Quigle, Lavender was constantly being called at work by Quigle, a media representative, volunteer or supplier. Such calls obviously took her away from patients; but they also required receptionists to answer the calls, locate Lavender and transfer the calls to her.

Early in the planning process Lavender spoke with Don Hastings, manager of the ProRehab clinic where she worked. Hastings talked with company owner Bill Franzen. Both were supportive; and agreed to let ProRehab clinics distribute flyers and serve as collection sites.

By mid-November the foundations of the Hugs & Kisses Project had been laid. But there was a long way to go. Few people knew about the project, no cards had been collected, and Lavender and Quigle had few ideas about where to get publicity, money, or organizational support.

A few weeks after first talking with television personality Randi Naughton Lavender called her again, to tell her "everything is in place." Two days later Naughton called back. Could Lavender be available to talk about her project at 7:20 AM next Tuesday? She could. The first media mention of the project, then, was on Fox 2 News' morning show on Tuesday, November 27th.

The evening before the Fox 2 appearance Lavender contacted a Landmark consultant on media affairs. The consultant's recommendation was to speak in ten- to fifteen-second sentences. Lavender spent the evening practicing. Portions of the morning show interview, surprisingly long, were repeated during the noon and evening newscasts.

The day before the Fox interview a local supermarket chain, Schnucks' Markets, had signed on to serve as collection sites. Schnucks not only agreed to collect cards at all stores, but to gather them at a central location to make it easier for Lavender to pick them up. The timing could not have been better: Lavender could not only describe her idea, but tell interested viewers where to take their cards.

Momentum was beginning to build, but there was little yet to show. When Lavender met a friend for breakfast at *La Bonne Bouchée*, a French bakery, early in December she had received only a handful of cards from one elementary school classroom. "I don't care," she said. "If I only get a hundred cards, I'll take a hundred cards to New York. Every little bit helps."

Nevertheless, Lavender was excited: another media "event" had been arranged, an interview with Nancy Quigle on radio station KMOX's popular morning news-magazine program. Lavender asked the waitress at *La Bonne Bouchée* if the restaurant's radio could be tuned to KMOX. Unfortunately, the *La Bonne Bouchée* sound system was limited to FM, so at the appointed hour (about 8:35 AM) Lavender and her friend ran to her car.

It was a short interview, of course — two or three minutes is a long time in the radio business. But it was another step, and Quigle had done a good job of describing the project's goals. Word was getting out.

Over the next two weeks media coverage mushroomed. Stories appeared in the *Post-Dispatch* on December 13th, and in a suburban weekly the following day. Other radio and television outlets began carrying the story. Fox 2 even read some of the cards Lavender had dropped off for them during their 6:00 AM newscast.

The original "end" of the collection period, December 15th, came and went. But publicity continued: An Associated Press writer called for an interview, and local television continued to cover the story. As a result, cards continued to pour in. Lavender's "idea" had developed its own momentum.

x o x o

Lavender had planned, all along, to visit her family in the New York area over the holidays; that is part of what made the Hugs & Kisses idea appealing and feasible. But now she was faced with the task of carrying – or shipping – a half-dozen large bags of cards as well.

Early on, Lavender had approached Southwest Airlines about options for transporting the cards to Hartford, Connecticut, her usual destination when she flew home. This was complicated, however, by concerns about anthrax, after several anthrax-laced letters were delivered through the US Postal Service.

Lavender solved these concerns by accepting only cards delivered without envelopes. With this assurance, Southwest agreed to transport the bags, and even offered two passes from St. Louis to Hartford. The flight was scheduled for Tuesday, December 20th, an early-morning flight with a stop-over in Chicago.

Lavender was not traveling to New York alone. As the project had gathered steam, several friends and Landmark associates had gotten involved, and made arrangements to make the trip. Sharon Rose and Phil Nouri, SELP participants, wanted to come; as did Mary Stephenson, Lavender's Landmark coach. Stephenson, a biologist who enjoyed taking pictures, became the groups' photographer. In addition, Sharon Rose's 17-year-old son, Will Flinner, and Phil Nouri's 10-year-old son Nick persuaded school officials that the trip would be educational and accompanied the group.

Ironically, Nancy Quigle was unable to make the trip.

Six people wearing baseball caps embroidered with the "XOXO" logo, and sitting together on an airplane, are bound to attract attention. Flight attendants had asked what they were doing, of course. Somewhat surprisingly, they announced the groups' presence and purpose to the rest of the flight. Fortunately, Lavender – never without blank cards – was able to distribute cards to fellow-travelers who wanted to participate.

The group's Tuesday night destination, dubbed "Hotel Hugs & Kisses," was the home of Deb's mother, Janet Schnitzher, in New Milford, Connecticut. Schnitzher, famous for her spaghetti, was able to feed and house the group, who spent the evening counting and photographing the cards.

Altogether, there were 6,343 cards.

And so it was that early – Sharon Rose was in the shower by 4 AM – on Friday morning, December 21st, 2001, the Hugs & Kisses group arrived in Lower Manhattan, driven by Alan Lavender and, dragging a dozen bags of cards, leaned into a cold west wind on their way to Battery Park.

And so it was that the small group of out-of-towners, faces reddened by the wind, bundled up in jackets and scarves and gloves, offered cards to harried commuters hurrying north from the Staten Island Ferry to Lower Manhattan office buildings.

Many, heading toward office buildings to the north, ignored the offerings with averted eyes. Others took one and hurried on. But once in a while someone would slow, reading what they had been given, and glance back with tears in their eyes.

X O X O

How valuable was the Hugs & Kisses Project?

For Deb Lavender it meant many things. It was a successful, completed, Landmark SELP project, of course. It provided an opportunity for Lavender and a surprisingly large group of friends, coworkers and colleagues to make a difference in a difficult and painful time. But more than anything, it provided an opportunity for many ordinary St. Louis men and women and boys and girls to have an effect, to be able to reach out and touch people – people they did not know but still cared about – hundreds of miles away in a city most of them had never visited.

And what about the recipients, those New Yorkers used to thinking of themselves as somehow separate and distinct from the vast midsection of the country? This is what a New Jersey commuter, who happened to get a card prepared by Lavender herself, later said:

On Sept. 11, my life was changed. I exited the PATH commuter rail station at the World Trade Center, and less than an hour later, watched as it crashed to the ground, taking 3,000 innocent lives with it. I witnessed death and destruction that I never ever thought imaginable on our soil. My life was forever changed by the events of Sept. 11. All our lives were. What I witnessed in the months that followed renewed my faith in humankind: spontaneous outpouring of warmth, kindness and love. Proof that we are all family.

On Dec. 21, I left my commuter ferry and was handed a homemade, handwritten Christmas card by a woman wearing a hat that said "XOXO." When I asked what it was, she simply replied "A Christmas card from St. Louis." I read the card and was nearly brought to tears. The card was signed by Deb Lavender of St. Louis. "Dear New Yorker, you are my hero. I honor your courage in continuing with your life. May you find peace during the holiday season."

I'll keep this card for all of my days. So little said so much. Merry Christmas Deb. And thank you.

Andrew Kleinwaks, Boonton, NJ. (*The Webster-Kirkwood Times*, January 11, 2002)

My Big Game:
A Latter-Day Coming of Age Story

Northof the big stone barn the ground fell away toward the road. Rocky and unfit for tilling, the hillside between the barn and the road was used as a holding area for pigs and cattle. As a slender teen I would spend hours every summer beside the barn, swinging a broomstick, methodically hitting my way through collections of rocks.

THWACK! "Scott swings, and it's a liner to left! Scottie rounds first and hustles into second with a double!"
THWACK! "Scott swings, and it's a long fly to left! It might be. . . it could be. . . it IS! A home run for the Scottster!"

I discovered baseball in 1947 when, at age nine, I began listening to St. Louis Cardinals' games on the radio. The Cardinals had won the World Series the year before — the last time they would do so for 18 years — and Harry Caray began each broadcast with his signature "home run" phrase: "It might be! It could be! It *is*! The *World Champion* St. Louis Cardinals are *on the air!*"

At the time we lived on a farm in central Missouri. I was the only child of less-than-social parents. Ira Hines Scott — actually my step-father, although I carried his surname — could be glib and charming,

95

but was essentially a loner. He and my mother met when they both worked in the same Detroit restaurant in 1941. After the war ended I. H. moved us to a central Missouri farm. In 1951 we moved again, to a larger place in the southwestern part of the state.

I. H. was not a big man, but he could be fierce. A professional boxer in his youth, he showed no fear; and I was sure that he was chronically disappointed in me. When I was four or five, while we still lived in Detroit, he brought home two pairs of boxing gloves. One pair was strapped on me; the second on Sharon, a cousin four months older. Within minutes she caught me on the tip of the nose with a well-placed punch, bringing me to knees and tears. My father took the gloves away, and I never saw them again.

But the consequences of the incident lingered. From that day on I knew I was a coward, too fearful to ever be acceptable to my father. I realize now that much of my fear resulted from overestimating his dangerousness, but as a child, of course, I could not understand that.

Tending toward paranoia, I. H. kept us isolated, pushing potential family friends away, a pattern that seemed agreeable to my mother. Gertrude Scott — called "Jean" by my father — was the kind of woman who would nervously tell other people things they neither needed nor wanted to know, and seemed to prefer isolation herself. By any standard, I was a child of overwhelmed and disinterested parents.

If it had not been for school I might have become trapped in this isolated world. Even so, I was unable to participate in after-school activities. Forced to ride a bus home, needed for chores and field work, I could never do the things that enriched my friends' childhoods. The eighth-grade schoolboy patrol, for example, which directed traffic before and after school, was unimaginable, as were high-school drama productions, rehearsed and performed in the evenings. Or, for that matter, after-school sports.

So, *my* sports were played in the privacy of my imagination.

⊘

For a lonely and isolated child Harry Caray's Cardinals broadcasts were magical, and I was soon hooked. My world came to revolve around the accomplishments of Stan Musial and Enos Slaughter and Red Schoendiest, with Caray's descriptions providing the pictures. Furthermore, riding tractors — plowing or cultivating — provided time alone and ambient noise for additional "broadcasts" that played in my mind.

"Runners on second and third, and Slaughter digs in at the plate. Here's the wind-up, and the pitch. . . Slaughter swings, and it's a line drive into the hole in right-center, and all the way to the wall. Two runs score! Slaughter's rounding second and heading for third. Here's the throw. . . Enos slides. . . and he's SAFE! The Cardinal's lead, three to two!"

Not surprisingly, for an imaginative child with little more than fantasy to work with, I soon injected myself into the pictures. When "Stan the Man" coiled into his unusual batting stance *it was me* lining the ball into the gap. *I* slipped on my glove on at the last possible instant and, like the Redhead at second, scooped up a grounder to fire to first for the third out. *I* raced around third and slid past the catcher, *ala* Country Slaughter, with the winning run. In the league within my head I was a *player*.

In the real world, however, I was a skinny and timid egghead with unruly hair and limited social skills, lousy at the only thing – sports — that *really* mattered.

To be honest, there *were* a few exceptions. In grade school, for a while, I was in demand as a goalie during pick-up soccer games. We played soccer at lunch in the school-yard. Having no actual nets — I'm not sure we even knew about nets — points were scored by kicking the ball over the opposing team's end-line. As goalie I'd roam side-to-side, or even race back and catch the ball over my head. As long as the ball did not hit the ground our rules said no goal was scored.

I *was* good, once called "the best damn goalie around." What the other players never knew was that *in my mind*, I wasn't playing goalie. I was *really* playing shortstop, the reincarnation of Cardinals' shortstop Marty Marion.

Time passed, however, and other activities replaced soccer after lunch. Goal-line successes faded from memory, and other moments, usually fleeting, were quickly forgotten. Like the time I snared a hot liner while at third base during a lunch-time game of "work-up."

"Work-up" was the way we played baseball when there weren't enough players for two teams. Fielders moved up one position each time an out was made, finally becoming one of three or four "batters." A batter making an out went to right field to begin "working up" again. In our version, a fielder who caught a ball on the fly immediately replaced the batter; so, my great catch meant something. But, as I coolly trotted toward the plate, the bell rang. When everybody headed for class it was as if my catch had never occurred.

But the Cardinals were always with me. I followed them, listening to as many games as possible all the way through school. I felt much more kinship to the voices I knew from the broadcasts than to my own family. I knew the players, the stats, and even learned about strategy.

My parents apparently understood and accepted this, even though I assumed I was being very private. My father even arranged for me to make two bus trips to St. Louis to see Cardinals games, amazing (and, looking back on it, foolish) acts of confidence in an immature teenager who didn't know the way to the neighbor's house.

One trip was with a group of baseball fans for "fan appreciation day," an event sponsored by the Cardinals. I recall getting Harry Caray's autograph, and sitting behind a post in Sportsman's Park next to a man becoming progressively more intoxicated as the game wore on. The next year I traveled on my own, flagging down a Greyhound as it passed a highway crossroad a few miles from our farm. I don't remember the game that year, but I do recall wandering around the dilapidated early-1950s riverfront area of St. Louis, and even going into an "adults-only" movie as I waited for the bus home.

Through it all my rich fantasy career in baseball continued. One always assumes, of course, that one's fantasies are private, so I was amazed one summer afternoon when my father, in a teasing voice, complained to my mother about my work on the tractor. "I can't let him cultivate," he said. "By the time Slaughter gets to third he's dug up half a row of corn!"

It *was* funny, of course, but scary as well. How the hell could he know what was going on in my head?

I would spend hours, on quiet summer days, firing a battered rubber ball against the cement porch steps. If the ball hit a step squarely it would bounce back, a grounder. If it caught a top edge it would be a fly. I could practice pitching, fielding grounders and catching fly balls all at the same time. This was, I was certain, the kind of training that made future big-leaguers.

"Ground ball to the hole. . . . GREAT stop by Scott. He turns and fires to first. . . . OUT! Holy Cow, what a play by the Cardinals' all-star shortstop!"

I always knew, of course, that I was never destined to be a ballplayer. Not only would I never have the opportunity, I did not have the talent. I was small and fearful, and I could hardly see, let alone hit, run or throw. Whatever future I had lay in using my head.

Or, perhaps, my mouth. Maybe I could be a sportscaster.

So, when I went away to college (to the Rolla School of Mines, Missouri's engineering school), I made a tentative reach for sports glory, broadcast-style, exploring getting hired by a local radio station. I had the voice for it, but the job required passing a difficult radio engineer's licensing exam, since small-town radio announcers had to run the station's equipment.

Shortly before the date for the engineer's exam I transferred to Baylor University in Waco, Texas, ostensibly to study to be a Baptist preacher but, perhaps, also to avoid having to take the engineer's test. The closest I came to sports in college was as a gymnasium maintenance worker, sweeping the floor during Baylor basketball games. (I once picked up a loose ball during half-time and arched a shot toward the basket. It missed, generating sarcastic applause.)

Life goes on, of course, despite uncompleted dreams. A man can find ways to adjust, to sublimate, or to pursue new dreams. In the process a man can often become a spectator, an observer of sports who asserts knowledge, if you will, despite having never played.

Life's twists took me to Los Angeles, where I worked for a bank, then as a welfare worker, and later (in an unlikely role for a grown "scared kid") as a parole officer. While there I tried to follow the Dodgers, but it was never the same. Once a Cardinals' fan, always a Cardinals' fan.

I did try out for a church league fast-pitch softball team in L.A., but I was still slow, weak-armed and hesitant. Worse, by then I had a paunch that interfered with swinging a bat or fielding a grounder.

Furthermore, softball — misnamed, because the ball can be just as hard as a baseball, only bigger — is every bit as fast as baseball, except that the bases are thirty feet closer. Unable to put the bat on the ball, I never got into a game, serving primarily as a bat-and-ball caddie.

More twists of life led east: to Southern Illinois for graduate school; then to Virginia for a college teaching job; and, finally, back to Missouri. Along the way I divorced one wife and married a second, and gave up one university position for another. My abortive interest in ministry, which had proven to be a step toward the helping professions and teaching, ultimately led me into psychology.

Only the Cardinals remained a constant. I did play a little tennis, but it was never the same. Even I could not fantasize competing with Jimmy Connors.

And I was *past forty*, getting old. If I was going to "make it," prove myself, it would never be on a diamond, or a field, or a gym floor. Being a psychologist did make it easier to begin the mid-life process of redefining masculinity: *feeling* became more important than *doing*. I even learned to embrace my "lack of athleticism" as a virtue.

Then I discovered slo-pitch.

$\oslash$

Church league slo-pitch softball is the perfect game for middle-aged "wanna-be" athletes. Where fast-pitch softball is a pitcher's game, with underhanded fastballs and curves almost impossible to hit, in slo-pitch the ball is served up in a tantalizing ten-foot arc. Because the ball is usually put in play by the batter, it is a game that puts a premium on defense but, played on a smaller diamond, is still easier on aging arms and legs.

We had been members of a suburban St. Louis church for a few years when I noticed a newsletter announcement about the formation of a slo-pitch team. I showed up at the organizing meeting with little optimism.

The organizer was a young high school teacher named Richard Martin, who had, I think, played a little college ball. At our first practice I was pleased to note that I was not the oldest man present. My hopes rose a little as we tossed the ball around and I was able to hit some pitches in batting practice.

But, of course, most of the other players were better than I, and in that first year, when I did get to play, it was in that dead zone for the hopeless athlete, right field. Even there, in the last game of the year, I waved helplessly at a long drive as it sailed over my head, costing us the game.

Things picked up a couple of years later, however, when more men joined the team and a "B" team was created. We played other church "B" teams, but our games counted in the final league standings. The primary effect was to separate out the better players, leaving a more level playing field (a questionable metaphor considering the diamonds we were using) for the rest of us.

On the "B" team, at least, I was assured of playing time. In fact, since we often barely had enough players for a team, anyone who was dependable was usually on the infield, and I was soon the regular first baseman. Since I had always been able to catch, I was able to handle the position fairly well; and missed balls (usually in the dirt or over my head) could be easily blamed on infielders' throwing.

After a few games at first base I volunteered to catch. Catching, in slo-pitch, is pretty unchallenging, with the arched ball bouncing just behind the plate and easy to catch. Furthermore, base runners are not allowed to steal, so slo-pitch catchers seldom have to throw any further than back to the pitcher. But to an old fantasizer, as catcher I was the *field general*, an integral part of the ("B" team) machine.

There is only one difficult play for a slo-pitch catcher: a throw to the plate when a runner is trying to score. Since most of the players in our league were reluctant to slide, and no one wore spikes, even that was usually pretty tame. Still, the day inevitably came when a burly runner, caught up in a youth he could not remember, came barreling toward the plate while the ball sailed toward me from the outfield. Not having time to think, I planted myself in front of the plate, caught the ball, and swiped my glove toward the sliding runner.

I missed him, of course, but the umpire couldn't see that in the confusion. The runner complained, but finally limped off, called out. Meanwhile, I fired the ball to the third baseman, a ritual I'd watched big leaguers do.

I don't really recall how I ended up pitching. I think Coach Martin, who usually pitched for both the "A" and the "B" teams, had to leave early one day, and asked me to take over. But surprisingly, I had a knack for pitching. I could arch the ball with height and still get it over the plate; could toss it inside or outside; and could even put a little spin on it. The result was that, while average players could usually hit it, they couldn't hit it very hard. After a while, I was the regular pitcher when Martin was away.

We still lost all our games, since our "B" team was not very good, but *I* was a player, a major cog, a *pitcher*. I would like to tell you I handled all this success with humility, but the truth was that I was incredibly proud. Furthermore, as the season wore on, I was pitching better. Pretty soon, Martin was not even getting to our games until they were half over.

There were times, of course, when I wondered what a forty-year-old man with allergy-blurred vision was doing tossing a ball signed "hit me" from only forty-five feet, but I was usually able to get the pitch where I wanted. Big hitters got outside balls and inside strikes, so they usually hit their longest shots foul. I only threw outside strikes to little guys. Even so, however, one batter *did* smash it up the middle, off my shin, leaving me limping for two weeks.

⊘

The fateful day, as it happened, was the next-to-the-last game of the season. I was pitching well, and the other team seemed disinterested. We scored a run in the second, and another in the fourth when, suggesting that a miracle was in the works, I hit a pitch over the left fielder's head, scoring a runner from first base. By the sixth inning they had had only six scattered hits, and had gotten no runner past second. We were on our way to a win — our first of the year.

"Scott leans forward on the mound, staring down at the big power hitter waving his bat menacingly. The crowd's on its feet as Scottie glances around. The bases are loaded, two men out, three and two on the batter. The games on the line as Scott goes into his windup . . .."

Well, all right — it wasn't so much a "mound" as a slight depression in the middle of the bare infield. And, for that matter, the "crowd" consisted of some half-dozen wives and girlfriends talking with each other and ignoring the game.

So, I was actually looking *up* at the batter, who was, in fact, a slender accountant from a neighboring church. And my wind-up was more a backswing, needed to toss the ball toward the plate with an arc.

And, if you must know, there really wasn't much on the line either. It was only the sixth inning of a seven inning "B" league church slo-pitch softball game. But we *were* ahead two to nothing, which in slo-pitch is no lead at all. So, it was a pretty tense situation, even with two outs and nobody on base. You just don't see shut-outs

104

in slo-pitch, and here *I* was, pitching one. Me. The ultimate athletic under-achiever.

Which was why, when our shortstop scooped up the accountant's little grounder and fired to first, I pumped my fist in the air. One inning to go! Can you blame me? I was finally getting my chance to shine.

Rich Martin arrived as we were batting in the top of the seventh. Our guys, charged beyond belief, scored two more runs as other players filled Martin in. I sat alone on the bench, playing the role of the concentrating pitcher, trying to look cool, as if I were used to such success.

As I started for the mound at the end of the inning Martin met me. Assuming he was planning to play first, a welcome defensive move, I said, "Four-zip, three outs to go, Rich. We've got this one!"

Martin picked up the ball, lying near the pitcher's rubber. "Good job, Scottie," he said, holding on to the ball. "I'll finish up."

I stood, dumbfounded, until he slapped me on the back and said, "Take first."

We lost, of course. Martin could not throw a strike at first, and he walked the first batter. Then there were three hits, including a double, and the lead was down to four to three, with a runner on second. My shut-out was gone; even the win was shaky. Another walk, and the winning run was on base. I picked up a grounder, but my only play was to Martin covering first, and the runners advanced. This time, the game really *was* on the line.

When Martin stabbed the one-hopper back through the middle, I broke for first, ready to celebrate our first win, willing to forgive the loss of my shut-out. But his throw was wide, and in the dirt, and it crawled up my arm, over my shoulder, and down the right field line. Suddenly *we* weren't celebrating. *They* were celebrating.

One by one, players from both teams offered consolation: "Good game!" "Hell of a game!" "You'll get 'em next week." Martin, obviously upset with his performance, could only mumble, "Tough loss," as he headed for his car.

I waited until I got home to cry.

⊘

It turned out that it rained the next week, and we never did play our last game. I'm not sure why — perhaps a distracting life-crisis — but I did not go out for the team the next year. I don't remember being all that upset about not playing. If you've never expected athletic success, I suppose, there's less incentive to keep trying to achieve it.

And, of course, I knew I *had* pitched a whale of a game.

But I have thought about it — my big game — from time to time. The experience did change the way I think about myself. I've spent less time contemplating my masculinity since that day. Of course, that may be no more than a normal consequence of aging.

I've even thought well of Rich Martin, whenever he's come to mind. After all, he did give me the chance to play, even if he screwed up my big game. And he *was* trying to do the right thing. He just "over-coached" a bit.

What I've come to understand, in the end, is something about that old cliché about winning and losing. It's never been about winning, you know, or even losing, for that matter. It's always been about playing.

We may have lost. But, for six innings on a hot St. Louis afternoon, *I* was a *player*.

Fables and Fantasy

The End of a Perfect Marriage:
A Fable

This is the way the perfect marriage of George and Lucinda Amberth came to an end: in the middle of the night, amid confusion and triviality.

Any reader who has been married, or was even born into a marriage, will know that a good marriage — to say nothing of a perfect one — is difficult to achieve and, perhaps, impossible to sustain. The wise reader will also know that a good marriage may, in the end, be more desirable than one that is merely perfect.

But Mr. and Mrs. George Amberth had indeed achieved that rare state, acknowledged by both of them, of marital perfection. For more than two years they had loved each other, enjoyed each other, and done things together, sharing likes, dislikes, hopes and dreams, and never ever arguing. At the end of every work day each hurried home to be with the other. They cooked, dined and cleaned together; they read or talked or watched television together; they even yawned, readied for bed and arose the next morning together. They, and all their friends, said that they were "perfect together."

This is not to say that they did not each have lives of their own: George often lunched or played racquetball with friends from his work; and Lucy also enjoyed chatting, or lunching, or early-morning walks with friends.

And so it was that the evening came when Lucy, having yawned in preparation for bed, mentioned to George that she was meeting a friend early the next morning for a walk.

"We have to walk early tomorrow," she said, "so I've set the alarm for 6:45."

George grunted in assent, although his thoughts were displeased, because he knew he would never be able to get back to sleep with his wife getting up that early. George Amberth was programmed to sleep until 7:30 AM, and any earlier arising would leave him weary during the day. Still, walking with her friend was important to Lucy, and so he crawled into bed without further comment.

After putting on her nightclothes and brushing her teeth Lucy Amberth crossed the bedroom to the clock radio on the dresser on the other side of the room, pressed a button or two, and then crawled into bed. Within moments both she and George were fast asleep.

George, who had always been quicker to awaken than Lucy, sat up abruptly when the radio came on. Still, he was unusually groggy. He looked across the room to the clock, which read 6:45. The radio, which had been tuned to the local National Public Radio station, presented the voice of an announcer with a British accent reading the "BBC World News." Still half asleep, George got out of bed and crossed the room to turn the radio off — no sense awakening Lucy, he thought — vaguely wondering why the usual morning NPR program, "Morning Edition," was not on.

Turning off the radio George picked up his watch from his dresser and, crossing into the bathroom, closed the door and turned on the light. The light temporarily blinded him, and he squinted to see the time: 12:47. He shook his head, and looked again. Still 12.47.

George returned to the bedroom and looked at the clock on the clock radio, which now read 6:48. Confused, he peeked through the closed window blind. It was dark outside. Lucy must have messed up the clock and reset the time by mistake, he thought.

Realizing that he had a headache, George remembered that he had taken aspirin at bedtime. It was too soon to take more. He decided to reset the clock and try to get back to sleep. Turning off the bathroom light he returned to the clock radio. Trying to reset the time without awakening Lucy, George felt along the top of the radio, searching for the reset button. He pressed a button, muttering "Damn!" when the radio again erupted. Frantically pressing buttons in the dark to try to turn the radio off served only to raise its volume alarmingly.

Becoming more awake by the minute, George struggled to consider options. If he turned the volume down they might sleep through the alarm in the morning, resulting in Lucy missing her walking date. But to reset the time he needed to be able to see; if he turned on the lamp beside the radio he would awaken Lucy for sure.

He felt along the dresser top for a flashlight, then remembered he had left a clip-on book light, to be able to read himself to sleep without bothering Lucy, on his nightstand. Finding it among a pile of books, magazines and crossword puzzles, he remembered that it had developed a faulty switch (which was why he no longer used it). As a result, he could not keep the light on and work the radio's buttons at the same time. Furthermore, in his sleep-deprived state he could not figure out how to turn the radio's "sleep" function off.

George was on his knees, pulling the dresser away from the wall, so he could unplug the radio and disconnect the sleep function, when Lucy finally awoke.

"What in the world are you doing?" she asked, irritation evident in her voice.

But George was well past irritation by this point. Silent at first, anger then tumbled out in a rush, voice rising as he talked: "You've screwed up the clock and I can't reset it," he hissed, "and I hit the snooze button by mistake and I can't figure out how to turn the damned thing off and so I pulled out the dresser to unplug the clock but I can't find a flashlight and so I can't see to plug the damn thing back in!"

"There's a flashlight right on the bookstand beside you."

There was, of course, but by now George Amberth was damned if he was going to use it. Feeling with his fingers he found the electrical receptacle and plugged the radio back in. The BBC came back on. There was, apparently, no way to disconnect the sleep function short of throwing the radio out of the bedroom window – an option he rejected only after serious consideration. Frustrated, he hit the "sleep" button again, realizing immediately that he had just added another 30 minutes to the BBC broadcast.

"Damn!" he said again, this time loud enough to be clearly heard.

"JUST LEAVE IT ALONE!" said Lucy, anger of her own boiling over.

"I'M DAMN WELL NOT GOING TO LEAVE THE DAMN THING ALONE!" George shouted in return. Then, deciding to leave it alone anyway, he stalked out of the bedroom, slamming the door as he went.

George could hear Lucy getting up to go to the bathroom as he walked through the darkened hall into the living room. Finding the remote, he turned on the television. As the screen brightened he found himself watching Jerry Springer, where a man with a ponytail was telling another man with a goatee that he had been sleeping with his – Goatee's – girlfriend. The two men began circling each other, warily. As Goatee pushed Ponytail the crowd began to applaud. George turned the television off.

He curled up on the couch, pulling the afghan over his feet, and tried to calm himself. From the bedroom he could hear the muffled sounds of the BBC. He was taking deep breaths, trying to find a pressure point to ease his headache, when Ming Yow, their nearly deaf 14-year-old calico cat, nuzzled his face.

It was the last straw, the act that put him over the edge. He hurled the poor old cat across the room, jumped up from the couch, and still in his underwear, rushed through the darkened apartment. Taking a short-cut through the dining room he rammed his bare toe against the table's leg, resulting in a creative string of shouted profanity that easily carried back to the bedroom.

Limping and cursing, George finally reached the kitchen. Filling a glass with ice he found a half-empty bottle of gin under the counter, poured the glass half-full, and added a can of V-8 from the refrigerator. Sitting at the table he gulped down half of the glass before realizing that it would probably make his headache worse. He was looking for aspirin when Lucy came to the kitchen door.

"What the hell is wrong with you?" Lucy asked. It was the first time George had ever heard her swear; still, he only glared. Abruptly she turned and went back to bed. George sat at the table for a few minutes before returning to the living room couch. Turning on the television again he watched the last half of an "All in the Family" rerun, then part of an even older "I Love Lucy" episode. Finally, verifying that the clock radio had finally turned off, he returned to bed. George tried to lie quietly, hoping the headache would go away, and finally fell asleep. Soon afterward Lucy began to softly snore.

Lucy avoided George the next morning until she was sure he had cooled down.

Finally, she said, "Are you feeling better?"

"I still have a little headache. I guess I don't do well when I wake up right after going to sleep," he replied.

"What happened to the radio?"

"I don't know — you must have messed up the time."

It was as close as either of them came to an apology.

But both realized that something was over, that somehow things would never be the same. No longer could they say they had a perfect marriage.

As George ate his cereal in silence and Lucy sat watching him, both felt waves of sadness.

Of course, George and Lucinda Amberth stayed together. Of course, they continued to love each other, enjoy each other, and do things together; even to yawn, prepare for bed and get up together. But they also experienced disappointments from time to time, some small and some large, sometimes individually, sometimes together.

By all reasonable accounts, they had a very good marriage.

As any reader who has been married, or even has been born into a marriage, will know, a good marriage – to say nothing of a perfect one – is difficult to achieve and, perhaps, impossible to sustain. But the wise reader will also know that a good marriage will, in the end, be much more desirable than one that is merely perfect.

Reverie

As was his custom, the old man finished his morning coffee and crossed to the sink, where he rinsed and left his cup. Glancing out a window to gauge the temperature, he took a light jacket from the rack by the back door. "Time for my morning walk, Blackie," he said, passing the cat sleeping on a chair.

Noticing the date on the kitchen calendar he went instead into the living room, stopping before a small framed picture on the corner table. "Nice legs," he said aloud, to no one in particular, a custom he had come to use to ease the loneliness.

He stared for a long moment at the people in the fading photograph. The man — himself — was a little over thirty, dark hair, clean shaven, surprisingly thin. "Where did I ever get that ugly brown suit?" His arm was around the waist of an attractive woman of about the same age. She was wearing a short white dress, fashionable at the time, which struck several inches above her knees. Beside them were twins, uncomfortable in matching outfits.

"How old were they then — about four?" Replacing the picture, he pulled his jacket on and went out the back door, locking it behind him. His mind wandered among memories as he slowly walked.

He had always thought that theirs had been an unlikely relationship, and that she was "out of his league." She was beautiful, desirable, and appeared much younger than she was. He was already given to paunch, and even though a year or so younger looked (and felt) much older.

Each, however, were coming out of failed marriages. She had the twins; he had three children living with an angry ex-wife. He had always wondered if she only needed him because of the twins; but he needed them too, to ease his own guilt. They had met, in the strange way these things happen, in a psychiatric hospital where she worked as a social worker. Despite the rumor, he always joked, he was not there as a patient, but as a graduate student, at the hospital on a three-month summer internship.

They had been married by a friend that also happened to be an Episcopal priest, at a lovely little chapel in the Illinois town where they lived, before some two-dozen friends. The twins participated in the wedding; his three were not present. (He remembered with amusement how Stephen, one of the twins, said "Cake!" — apparently his primary recollection of the day — later as he passed the church.)

Later the group gathered at a restaurant — what was it called? Petite New Orleans? – in a nearby town. It was a festive occasion, he remembered — good food, good wine, good friends — but he also remembered feeling uncomfortable, disquieted. "After all," he said aloud, "I knew for sure was that I didn't know the first thing about how to be married."

Could it really have been fifty years ago today? "And they said it couldn't last!" he chuckled aloud, again to no one in particular.

He wanted to recall their life together as completely blissful, but he knew that it was not. They had moved — from Illinois to Virginia (a move, he remembered, she had not wanted to make), and then back to the Midwest, to St. Louis. There had been good times, of course; but difficult ones as well (most of them, in his judgment, of his making).

They had even been separated for a few months. The fact that they survived that difficult period had made its memory no less painful for either one of them. Perhaps, he mused, painful memories are necessary for the growth of grace and love.

In the beginning he did not believe that she could love him – or, for that matter, that anyone could — and wondered, in his dark moments, why she married him. It took him years — too many years – to learn the obvious: that his concerns about her feelings were actually shadows within himself, shadows of his inability to love himself.

Fortunately, he never knew what she thought in the beginning. But, as time itself attested she persisted, waited. Perhaps, in her own way, she prayed. Whatever she did, it worked. One day, suddenly, in the manner that gradual truth dawns, he realized that the answers to his doubts and fears lay where he was — or, more accurately, where she was. It was one of those quietly cataclysmic moments when he realized that he loved her very much, that he wanted to be married, and, greater miracle yet, that he was loved.

It was the moment when he began to understand love.

The old man's memory raised the image of a majestic mountain scene he had once seen on a poster in a Sunday School classroom, with the caption, "Miracles take a long time!" Over the years the poster had come to carry layers of meaning for the man: for the nature of life, for love, and especially for his marriage.

He had come to understand that love had more to do with acceptance than with expectations, with respect than with certainty, with persistence than with passion. Love, he had come to understand — true, lasting, growing love — is much more about time than temperature.

So, what does an old man do, on the occasion of the 50th anniversary of his marriage, to express the love he feels? What can he do when he grew old learning not to express, especially when his feelings were so strong that he feared he could not show them without losing control? How could such a man tell his wife — especially when she is no longer here — how much he loved — loves — her, and how glad he is that she persisted long enough for him to finally figure it out?

He tells himself a love story.

Izabel's Adventure

I t was just a game, really.

The game was to dart toward the open door, to see how close you could get before the door closed. Izzie loved to play games. And she was very curious. But she really didn't want to get Out.

Usually, the Person going through the door would close it before she got close. Sometimes, they would point a finger and speak in a loud voice. Once in a while, another Person would pick her up and hold her until the door closed. Or she might find a big foot in her way, pushing her back. But she never really wanted to get Out.

At first, Izzie wasn't sure what had happened. The door opened. She darted toward the door. The door closed. But something was different. Then she realized: she was outside of the closed door.

It was exciting at first. It was dark. Since Izzie was totally black (except for the small white patch on her throat), she was almost totally invisible. The Person who had gone outside did not see her, did not know she had gotten out. She would be able to explore, to have fun. It would be Izzie's adventure!

$$\star \quad \star \quad \star \quad \star \quad \star$$

Outside was wonderful!

It was huge, much larger than she had realized. She had never been Outside, except when the big Person with the hairy face carried her out to pick up the thing he called the "paper."

Izzie explored along the wall, around the corner. She recognized smells: the big Thing that made noise and rolled by itself, which was sometimes in the place the Persons called "Garage," where she loved to play.

She found the familiar smell of the other Person who sometimes came to feed her when her Persons were away. And the animal who lived in the next Place and made so much noise when Izzie stared at her through the window.

But soon Izzie had explored beyond familiar smells, down a hillside, into tall grass and trees. There were so many new scents, new places. And Izzie was very curious. She wandered among the trees, crouching In the tall grass. She stalked the smells of the flying things she had seen through the window, not realizing that they were all asleep in the trees.

Instinctively, Izzy tried to climb a tree. But it was hard: Izzie had had her front claws removed because she shredded furniture. She wandered further down the hill. Then she found water. The water, moving past her, smelled and tasted fresh. But it was much too wide to get across. She began walking along the stream, exploring. Izzie enjoyed being curious.

It was some time before she realized she was lost. She had assumed a Person would come to get her. She had expected to hear her name, to be picked up, to be carried back inside. But no one came.

After a while, Izzie decided to go back. But she did not know where back was, and she recognized no smells. She knew, somehow, that she had to go up the hill; and sure enough, she came to a big Place. This Place certainly was big enough to have an Inside; but there were no familiar smells. Wandering around the Place, Izzie came to a door. She sat, and began to scratch. But no one came to let her in.

Izzie realized she was cold. She became frightened. She began to squall. But no one came. Tired and frightened, she finally curled up in a corner and fell asleep.

⁎　　⁎　　⁎　　⁎　　⁎

Izabel woke up when she heard noises coming from inside the Place. She began to scratch on the door, but no one came. She cried out, but the door did not open. Then she heard a loud noise. Frightened, she ran around the corner, hiding in a bush.

A huge door was rolling up, making the loud noise. One of the Things that rolled by itself, also making noise and spouting bad smells, began to roll out. The door came back down. The Thing rolled away.

Frightened, Izzie ran down the hill, and found the tall grass again. But this time it was totally different. It was light, and she could see. With a start, she realized she could also be seen. She crouched, hiding.

The grass was teeming with activity. Small Creatures crawled, jumped, flew. Izzie had always enjoyed chasing such Creatures when she was Inside. But Inside, there would only be one or two creatures. Here, there were so many. It was so curious, but frightening.

Then she saw the Flying Thing, called "Bird." Somehow, Izzie had always known she should pursue birds. Instinctively her tail began to twitch. She was so intent she did not see the other bird behind her. But it saw her.

The second bird, protecting his mate, swooped down on the small cat, screeching. Suddenly terrified, Izzie raced down the hill, leaped into a clump of tall grass, and hid, panting. She stayed in the grass for hours.

Eventually, hunger overcoming her fear, she ventured out. It was quieter now, and warmer, with less activity. She looked for something to eat. But she had no idea where to look. She had always found food beside the big Thing where the People kept their food; but that was Inside. And she was Outside.

She could find water, though. A little way down the hill, she found the stream again. The water was cool, and tasted fresh. The water was better Outside than Inside, she thought. But where could she find food?

A jumping creature appeared, and, without thinking, Izzie pounced, grabbing it with her mouth, swallowing. It tasted strange, but it was food. She looked for more.

It was hard work, and not very good tasting, but it helped. She discovered that some Creatures were easier to catch than others, and some tasted better than others.

Eventually, tired, she curled up in some grass and fell asleep.

*   *   *   *   *

When she awoke, Izabel realized it was dark again. She was cold, and wet. Drops of water were falling around her. Soon she was soaked, the water falling very hard. Izzie huddled in the tall grass, trying to stay warm, and trying to stay dry.

The water continued to fall, and eventually, cold, hungry and frightened, Izzie fell asleep again.

*   *   *   *   *

When she again awoke, the water had stopped falling, and it was beginning to become light. But the grass was still wet, and it was cold.

Activity was beginning. Crawling Creatures were moving about, and birds were beginning to call to one another. Even though she was frightened, Izzie was too hungry and cold to stay hidden. Cautiously, she began to move about.

She caught a few Crawlers. Then she came upon a small, furry animal lying on the ground, under a tree. It did not move, and did not run away. Without thinking, without knowing why, Izzie ate the baby mouse.

As she continued to wander, Izzie gradually felt less fearful. Her exploring was not so much because of curiosity anymore, though, but to find out how to keep safe, and how to get food. She remained close to the stream, gradually widening her circle of exploration.

During the day she occasionally came upon food, and she felt less hungry. She felt more confident. If this was going to be home, perhaps she could survive after all.

But that was before It came.

It was huge, somewhat like the Animal that had lived next door when she lived Inside, and had made so much noise when she looked through the window.But this Animal was MUCH bigger. At first it did not make a sound. It was brown, with long shaggy hair. And it knew Izzie was there.

And suddenly, terrifyingly, it was racing toward her, growling. Izzie bolted, racing toward the stream. A tree appeared in her path, and, without thinking that she could not climb, using only her rear claws, she raced up the trunk to a safe branch. Panting, shaking, she huddled on the branch.

Even after the Animal wandered away Izzie, still afraid, stayed in the tree. Finally, it began to get dark. Carefully, cautiously, she jumped down.

*   *   *   *   *

That night Izzie continued to widen her circle of exploration. Despite her earlier fright, she was feeling somewhat more confident.

Since her People were gone, she would have to find out how to survive on the Outside, on her own.

So, she was surprised when she came upon a Place.

It seemed familiar, like the other Places she remembered, but there were no familiar smells. Nevertheless, she wandered along the sides of the Place, and came upon other, similar Places.

It was frightening, but it was dark, and it was quiet, so she continued to explore. Perhaps she could find some food. So, she was not expecting to discover something familiar.

It was a familiar smell. After a moment, she recognized it as the scent of the Person who sometimes fed her when her People were away. She found a door, and began to scratch. When no one came, she began to cry. Finally, she fell asleep.

$$* \quad * \quad * \quad * \quad *$$

She awoke when the loud noise, the big door rising, began. It was just becoming light. Frightened, she ran around the corner, and down the hill into the tall grass.

For two days Izabel explored, learning about her new home. She became more proficient at catching food. She learned to recognize when danger was near. She spent most of the light-time asleep in the tall grass.

One day, she heard loud crashing. She was not frightened, but still hid in tall grass. She knew she could not be seen, but to be on the safe side she remained hidden.

So, she did not see the Person – the big Person with the hairy face – as he looked for her. Only later, as it began to become dark, and as she began to move about, did she recognize the scent.

Somehow, the smell of her Person brought crashing back all her fears, all her loneliness. Cold, hungry, and frightened, she climbed back up the hill. Once again, she found the Places.

And once again she found the Place with the scent of the Person who sometimes fed her. Again, she scratched, and again she called, but no one came. She was about to give up, to run back down the hill, when the Rolling thing came.

⋆   ⋆   ⋆   ⋆   ⋆

But this Rolling Thing did not roll into the garage. It stopped a short distance away, across a strip of hard ground. And a Person got out.

Somehow, the Person seemed familiar. Even though Izzie knew she should be frightened and should run away, she still called out. The person walked nearby, toward another Place. He walked past the side of the Place toward the Inside.

Suddenly very frightened, Izzie called frantically. But she knew it was hopeless; she would have to live forever on the outside, alone. Slowly, hopelessly, she began to go back down the hill.

She was so disappointed she did not hear the Person, who lived In the Place with the Person with the hairy face, as he came back around the side of the Place. She did not hear him say "Izzie?" So, she was totally surprised when she was suddenly lifted up, and held in the Person's arms.

⋆   ⋆   ⋆   ⋆   ⋆

She was surrounded by familiar scents, textures and sounds. The person said, "Izzie? Is this you?" Almost immediately, she was inside. She was Inside! And she knew it was her Place!

Shaking, crying, she raced around, smelling familiar scents. Abruptly, she discovered her food dish. Food! She had not realized how hungry she was. She stopped, and ate, and ate. And ate.

Afterward, she found a familiar chair, and fell asleep.

*   *   *   *   *

The next morning Izzie awoke, unsure where she was. Initially she was frightened. Then she saw the other Person, the smaller one, the one who usually fed her.

"Izzie! You're home!" Excited, the Person swooped down on her, lifted her and began to pet her. "Look who is home!" she called out.

"Izabel! Where have you been?" Suddenly Izzie was being held by the bigger Person, the one with the hairy face. Except that this time the hairy face was wet, with tears.

But Izabel did not say where she had been. She never did say anything about her adventure. She did not have to. Izabel was home.

And she was very happy to be there.

Short Shots

Basement Legacy *

S hortly after moving to Calhoun County a few months ago we entertained dinner guests. The conversation included "moving discoveries" — things unearthed in the process of changing homes.

"We have these two violins," I commented, "that were buried in the basement of our in-town house. We're trying to figure out what to do with them."

Both violins had been rescued from our mothers' houses when they moved into nursing homes; and both were carted to our basement and forgotten. My wife recalls using her mother's violin when she took lessons in high school. My (vague) recollection was that my mother had also played in high school.

And so it was that the four of us gathered in our new basement, where I retrieved the two violins. The first, from Marilyn's mother, was better looking: richer, with a nice grain and good finish. *My* mother's violin looked . . . well, *cheap.*

Our dinner guest, who knew a little about such things, turned the nicer-looking violin this way and that, and even peered into the curved opening in the front. "Sometimes the maker signs his work on the inside," she said; "but I don't see anything in this one."

---

* This story first appeared in the December, 2003, edition of the Newsletter of the St. Louis Psychological Association.

Peering into the opening of the second violin she squinted, shifting the instrument to catch the light of the hanging bare bulb. "Something is printed in here," she said. "I see what looks like a 'T.' Let's see . . . looks like T - O – N – I – V - S." She pronounced each letter separately. "Then there's another word: S – T – R – A - D . . . ."

The full script, stenciled onto the base and carefully read with the aid of a flashlight, was:

Antonivs Stradiuarivs Cremonensis
Faciebat Anno 1719

Antonio Stradivari was born in 1644 near Cremona, Italy. At about 14 he was apprenticed to Niccolo Amati, a master violin maker. Within a few years he began producing his own instruments. Stradivari, who is known to have made at least 1,116 instruments, including some 540 violins, 12 violas and 50 cellos, did his best work from about 1700 to 1725. His genius lay in careful craftsmanship: interiors and exteriors remarkable in their precision. He also fixed the shape and position of the violin's sound-holes and bridge to produce the best quality of sound.

The very name, "Stradivari," designates the best in violins, and many of his instruments continue to be played today

Life provides far more questions than answers, of course. Was this battered violin, salvaged from my mother's closet, what it appeared to be? If so, how could my mother, a depression-era child, have come upon it? For that matter, did she have any idea what she had?

I did recall Mother once commenting that her violin "might be valuable," so perhaps she did know. But if so, where did it come from? Many questions, but few answers: Mother, currently residing in Bethesda Dilworth's Alzheimer's unit, wasn't going to be able to help.

Of course, Mother was part of a larger, talented family. One of my relatives is Rabbi James Stone Goodman (Mother's maiden name was Stone), who's great-great grandfather was my great-grandfather's brother. Goodman, a talented musician, likes to say that everyone in his family "either became a musician or a Rabbi." Goodman turned out to be both, of course, but somehow the musical gene skipped my branch of the family.

So, I couldn't help but let my imagination run. What if a *really good* violin came into the family's hands in Poland? Suppose it was passed down from one family member to another, and finally carried to America when family members emigrated in the early 1900s. It *could* have ended up in my basement, couldn't it?

Wouldn't *that* be a legacy for an old woman with Alzheimer's?

It isn't a real "Strad," of course. We showed the two violins to a friend, Janet Boyer, who for years sold classical and folk instruments as the owner of "Music Folk" in Kirkwood. Janet examined both violins carefully, even managing to extract a little sound with one of the old bows.

Marilyn's mother's violin had a nice sound, and would be "a good student violin," Janet said. My mother's violin was most certainly *not* a Stradavari. "You'd be amazed how many fake Strads are out there," Janet said. Apparently, putting the label of a famous instrument-maker in a violin has long been common.

Well, so much for imagination. Or, for that matter, for legacies. Still, in the end, aren't the most important family legacies really *stories*? There *are* stories here, even if Mother can't share them.

For that matter, why can't legacies be questions?

Rocky, Emma and the Bard: On Finding Love in Pekin*

Pekin, Illinois is some 200 miles from southern Calhoun County, depending on the route one chooses. We chose the scenic route, north through the county, with bluffs to our left and the Illinois River to our right. Even so, much of our drive was across Illinois flatlands, some of the richest soil on earth, but also some of the most boring.

But this trip was about the Bard, not scenery. We were making the overnight trip to Pekin to see grandson Andrew in his first high school play, Shakespeare's *Much Ado about Nothing*. Andrew, apparently inheriting my "self-minimizing" gene, had suggested that his role was "not very big; only one of the fathers." But it *was* a speaking part, and who wouldn't want to see a grandkid doing Shakespeare?

We pulled into Pekin about 4:00 PM, rested a bit at the EconoLodge, and headed to the house. Ringing the doorbell – a big mistake, we were later told – resulted in what sounded very much like a stampeding Clydesdale, followed by someone – or some*thing* – crashing into the inside of the front door. This proved to be Rocky, our grand-boxer, whose Pavlovian response to the sound of the doorbell is to attack the door.

---

*This story first appeared in the May, 2006, edition of the Newsletter of the St. Louis Psychological Association

Rocky's intent, however, is anything but hostile. He *is* excitable, to be sure; but he is affectionate to a fault and, despite being some 60 pounds of sleek, squirming muscle, is convinced he is a lap-dog. To be loved by Rocky is, indeed, a challenging physical experience.

As the family began to gather at the end of the Friday workday, we accompanied son Bob, grandson Grayson, and Rocky on the three-block walk to pick up granddaughter Emma from preschool. Rocky set the pace on the way to Emma's school, with Grayson holding on to his leash for dear life; while Emma controlled the return trip.

Emma joined the family about three years ago, adopted from her native China. From the beginning Emma has been a mixed blessing: beautiful and bright, she can be delightfully charming; but she is a strong-minded child and, at times, quite oppositional. Emma needs – no, *insists* – on being the center of attention, and can be demandingly affectionate. Together, Emma and Rocky can only be described as exhausting.

Much Ado about Nothing is something of a Shakespearean sit-com, a romantic comedy about the trials and tribulations of falling in love. The Pekin High School production was based on the 1993 movie version directed by Kenneth Branagh, starring Branagh, Emma Thompson, Denzel Washington and Michael Keaton.

The storyline, for the Shakespeare-challenged (as am I), involves a group of friends gathering in the home of Leonato (Andrew's role), a wealthy nobleman of Messina, Italy. Claudio, a visiting soldier home from war, quickly falls in love with Hero, Leonato's beautiful daughter. She reciprocates, and they decide to marry.

Meanwhile, Benedick, a family friend also returning from the war, resumes a long-standing bickering relationship (read "Harry and Sally" here) with Beatrice, Hero's cousin. These two insist they will never marry, but are soon tricked into believing that the other secretly loves them, resulting – you guessed it – in Benedick and Beatrice pledging *their* love to each other.

There are more high-jinks and hints of tragedy: Claudio is tricked into believing that Hero is running around on him, and abandons her at the altar. The family tells Claudio that Hero, who was innocent of his charges, has died of grief, and insists that he marry Leonato's niece (who looks a lot like Hero). Guilt-ridden, he agrees, only to discover at the altar that it really is Hero. In the end, in Shakespeare as on television, love wins out.

But life is not a sit-com, and real love is never neatly wrapped up by the closing credits. Real love is an evolving thing, whether it begins quickly, as in "at first sight," or over time, emerging out of a bickering friendship (or, for that matter, in a "legal" transaction, as in meeting your new child in an orphanage in China). Real love involves excitement, certainly, but also disappointment, and often anger and grief as we explore and change and grow together.

It is apparent, watching Bob, Linley, Andrew and Grayson with Emma, that there is "real love" there; but it seems never to be easy.

Real love may be "much ado," but it is never "about nothing."

Thomas Hunter*

The most entertaining gift we received this holiday season was from our son, Greg, and daughter-in-law, Robin, who live in Jacksonville, Florida. Arriving in a Hickory Farms box was a lovely basket containing big bags of Fartless 16 Bean Soup and Fartless Chili Makin's, to be served in a huge soup cup containing a 1736 quote from Benjamin Franklin: "Diligence is the mother of good luck, but he that lives for hope alone, dies farting."

We haven't had a chance to try the product yet, so we cannot personally attest to its accuracy in labeling; but we've had a lot of fun talking about it.

We had a chance to see Greg and Robin a few weeks earlier, at Thanksgiving, when we made a quick trip to northern Florida to see them and another son and daughter-in-law, Bob and Linley (and grandkids Grayson and Emma) in their new home in Palatka. They had relocated this past summer after Bob was named senior pastor of the First Presbyterian Church in Palatka.

Actually, Greg and Robin had news at Thanksgiving, having just learned that they were expecting their first child. What made this news particularly exciting was the fact that the baby – a boy – was due any day.

---

*This story first appeared in the January, 2008, edition of the Newsletter of the St. Louis Psychological Association

137

Talk about anxiety! We accompanied them one evening while they hurried through a baby store adding soon-to-be-needed things to their "wish list." But one of their first tasks needed to be to clean out the spare bedroom, which needed to be hurriedly converted into a baby's room.

Greg and Robin had been "expecting" for over a year already, having been placed on the waiting list for adoption of a daughter from China. But Chinese adoptions have become much more restrictive and slower in the last year or so, and certainly more so compared to Greg and Robin's brother and sister's experiences when they adopted Emma, now six, from China. (For the thoroughly confused, my sons Bob and Greg married sisters, Linley and Robin.)

During the past couple of years, then, Greg and Robin have been on a list of interested applicants for local adoption in Jacksonville, using a new, open, procedure. A coordinating attorney brings applications of interested couples to pregnant women interested in adopting their babies out. The birth mothers (sometimes aided by the birth fathers) review the applications, interview "finalists," and make a selection.

As you can imagine, the process is full of emotion for the birth mother and anxiety for the applying couples. Things could go wrong at the last minute: for example, the birth mother (or father) might change her (or his) mind, or there might be a problem with the birth, or the baby. But, as I suggested to Greg, "Parenthood is full of anxiety; you might as well get used to it."

In this case JoAnn, the birth mother (not her real name), seemed clear about her decision. Still rehabbing from a serious illness and a caregiver for her own disabled mother, JoAnn – more mature herself at 36 – seemed to understand that she would not be able to care for a baby. Besides, she liked Robin and Greg – she even brought them a stuffed animal (for the baby) at one pre-birth interview.

Here's the *really* exciting part. Thomas Hunter Scott, weighing in at seven pounds, no ounces, was born at 6:00 PM EST in Jacksonville. Robin was in the delivery room, and cut the umbilical cord. Greg, pacing a few yards away, was invited in shortly after the birth to give the (very unhappy) baby his first bath. Is this a wonderful world, or what?

There's still anxiety, of course. Greg and Robin are trying to adjust to parenthood – no sleep, worry about every peep and squawk (everything is new for them!) – and new information has required opening an investigation into possible whereabouts of the (previously unidentified) birth father. If he is located, he could throw a wrench into the adoption proceedings.

But it's looking as if he will not be found. And so, it's looking as if Thomas Hunter, grandchild number eight, will be in the middle of Thanksgiving next year. I've already sent him his first Cardinal's outfit.

The Yin and Yang of Things *

Father's Day weekend promised to be an enjoyable combination of baseball and family. Steve and Michele were driving in from Kansas City, and Steve and I had tickets for the Cardinals – Royals game Friday evening. Stephanie and Doug were coming Saturday, and we would all be together for a "Father's Day" lunch before Steve and Michele returned to Kansas City. Steve had to work the early show at Fox 4 television Sunday morning, and they wanted to get home in time to pick up Otis, our grand-basset, from a friend's house where they had left him Thursday evening.

Steve called Friday morning about 8 AM. "I want to tell you Otis died last night." Otis had gone to sleep Thursday evening; about 1:30 AM their friend Eleanor found him dead. Steve and Michele were "pretty broken up;" Eleanor was beside herself.

Steve and Michele had adopted Otis eleven years ago, while living in South Carolina. He was a good dog: gentle, loving, with huge floppy ears and an ever-present drool, always ready to eat, and with a bark that would frighten a burglar a block away.

Steve and Michele decided to come to St. Louis anyway; spending the weekend in an Otis-empty house seemed too depressing.

---

*This story first appeared in the July-August, 2011, edition of the Newsletter of the St. Louis Psychological Association

As it developed, however, we did not go to the baseball game: the river gods, who always seem to know when I have (expensive) tickets to some event, sent a six-foot wall of water down the Mississippi (and boosted the Illinois past flood stage as well). Driving to and from the game would add some five hours travel time, so we watched the Cardinals lose on our big-screen TV.

There is a yin and yang to life: good things happen, and bad things happen, not because of some cosmic system of justice, but just because of the way the world works. Life, whether of a fruit-fly, or a loving dog, or you and me, includes death. The miracle of consciousness brings also the awareness of suffering and loss. Human-kind's capacity for creation, morality and love also includes a capacity for anger, fearfulness and evil. The wise person understands this, accepts it, and integrates both into their reality.

Marilyn and I live in Calhoun County, Illinois, a beautiful rural area hard by the metropolitan area. Nestled between two great rivers, Calhoun features bluffs and hills on the Mississippi side, and green bottom land alongside the Illinois. The romance of southern Calhoun is enhanced by ferries, the only practical means of access from Missouri or the rest of southwest Illinois. Our villa sits atop a bluff above the Mississippi. We have a breath-taking view.

But when the river is high, or frozen, the ferry can't run, and the trip to town becomes longer. *Thirty to sixty miles* longer, depending on what route is available. And then, the Golden Eagle closes most nights at 9 PM, again lengthening any emergency-care trip across. As a depressed client observed when he learned we had moved to Calhoun County, "You know, your life expectancy will be lower over there!"

And so, it is that Marilyn and I expect to move into the newly completed Aberdeen Heights senior residency complex in Kirkwood this fall. Part of wisdom, as Kenny Rogers sang, is knowing when to hold 'em, and when to fold 'em.

Yin and yang.

The weekend before Father's Day three-year-old Thomas, together with his parents Greg and Robin, came from Florida to visit. Thomas is bright, extremely verbal, too cute by half, and has a healthy (and sometimes demanding) sense of self. They had a great (albeit tiring for grandparents) visit: The Magic House, City Gardens (on a 98° day!), even the Spaghetti Factory. On Sunday Thomas and his favorite grandparent Mari ("Marilyn" is too much for three-year-old mouths) were having a ball in the clubhouse pool, using water weights as battleships, when Thomas stopped and ran to Greg.

"Daddy, something bit me!" The red circle on the bottom of his big toe rapidly became inflamed. And as the toxin began to take effect, Thomas began to wail. Whatever he had encountered – bee? fire ant? – was *very* painful. Thomas cried off-and-on the rest of the day.

By the next day, Thomas was running again, albeit gingerly. "Popper," he said to me ("Papa Ron" is also a mouthful), "my boo-boo is better today!"

Yin and yang. Life – the good life – must contain both.

Old White Finds a New Home *

S everal years ago, Marilyn and I visited the Farnsworth Museum in Rockland, Maine. The Farnsworth houses the Wyeth Center, which displays three generations of the iconic Wyeth family art: illustrations by N.C. Wyeth; watercolor and egg tempera paintings by his celebrated son Andrew; and oils and portraits by Andrew's son Jamie.

I was drawn in particular to the simplicity and serenity of Andrew Wyeth's depiction of his New England world, best shown in such works as "Christina's World," a 1948 painting of a woman on the ground in an open field, reaching out and looking up at a house on the horizon.

A few weeks later, browsing through a catalogue of gift items, I found a framed print of another Wyeth painting, "Master Bedroom," a simple picture of a dog curled up on a bed, asleep with its head against the pillows. The bare room is unadorned. Sunlight streams across the bed through a single window, through which a tree is visible.

I showed the picture to Marilyn. "This would make a nice picture for the bedroom wall."

She was unimpressed. The print was large, expensive, and colorless. "It would be cheaper to buy a dog and let it sleep on the bed." Being, ultimately, a practical sort, I let the idea drop and forgot about the picture.

———

*This story first appeared in the December, 2011, edition of the Newsletter of the St. Louis Psychological Association

A few months later, at Christmas, we were opening gifts when she pointed to a rather large package I had not noticed leaning against the couch. As I began to carefully tear away the paper (sizable enough to be worth saving), I was dumbfounded to discover the once-coveted Wyeth print. I was moved to tears.

Master Bedroom has hung on my office wall in our riverside house for the past ten years. I have always found the sleeping dog, who I have named "Old White," comforting and inspiring, an image of comfort and belonging. But it is large: 35" by 30" framed, clearly much too big for a small apartment's wall.

There are many good reasons for moving into a "lifetime care" senior residential community like Aberdeen Heights, but have no doubts, it is a major lifestyle change. The sheer size and décor of the facility is very much like a luxury hotel. Hallways and the commons area are adorned with artwork. Meals are eaten in a lovely dining hall, served by attractive and well-trained young people who take our orders, bring delicious food to our table, and later clear away our dishes. Housecleaning changes our bedding and vacuums weekly. Maintenance hangs our pictures and changes our light bulbs.

In such an environment, it is important to make one's apartment as familiar as possible. Not surprisingly, almost everyone brings more furniture and furnishings than they can use. We spent a lot of time measuring and fitting specific pieces into uncertain spaces. Some pictures were selected, but among the most uncertain of spaces are walls.

We liked our "Mimosa" floor plan (all apartment designs at Aberdeen were named for trees) because the kitchen was in the rear of the apartment, with a window overlooking trees to the west. When we moved in, we discovered in addition that the design offered interesting nooks and angles, and – most appealingly – plenty of wall space. Enough space, as it turns out, for Old White to join us.

146

What makes a house – or, in this case, an apartment – a home? Familiar furniture, to be sure. Familiar faces, as well, speak of caring and belonging. But in a real sense, I believe, the things we hang on the wall provide the warmth, depth, and emotional tone of a space. Paintings provide color and texture; photos define family and history; plaques tell of lives well lived. A home's *story* can be found on its walls.

There is a story, of course, behind Andrew Wyeth's "Master Bedroom." But the story of the painting as it hangs in *our* second bedroom/office at Aberdeen lies in the meaning behind its presence.

It is, I know, a story of love.

In Pain in the Midst of Comfort*

There is a man in our community (and by "community" I mean our mental health community) who is understandably distressed. He has a child, a middle-aged adult child, who is by all appearances mentally ill.

This man recognizes that he is not unique. Many of us were drawn to this field because of experiences with a family member, or close friend, with a mental illness. We understand, in ways not learned from textbooks or seminars, or from work in psychiatric hospitals or clinical offices, the peculiarities of mentally ill behavior, the resistances to treatments we know will help, or the difficulties in maintaining treatment regimens.

Medication side effects are often unpleasant, while mania, as an example, feels invigorating. Fears that underlie many – if not most – mental illnesses also inhibit agreeing to treatment. There is a kind of freedom in differentness, despite the complications differentness produces.

This man's daughter communes with spirits: some identified, some not; some powerful, some less so; some familial. She receives regular spiritual instruction from a spiritual teacher, appearing to observers to be in trance. She is, she says, a medium, one who communicates with deceased persons' (such as Nelson Mandela's) spirits. She not only believes in reincarnation, she spends time processing traumas of some of her past lives.

---

*This story first appeared in the February-March, 2014, edition of the Newsletter of the St. Louis Psychological Association

So, the man struggles: with helplessness, since his daughter is a world away (and since, he knows, he would be helpless even if she were nearby). With worry, since the man knows that persons taking "direction" from someplace internal or beyond may engage in dangerous behavior. With guilt, since as a well trained and experienced mental health professional he thinks he should have seen this coming, should have been able to head it off, should be able to fix it.

The man finds it difficult to talk of any of this with others. Perhaps this is because he feels shame, a vestige of stigma not yet overcome. But he also fears the reactions of others who, not wanting to hear such things, might only feign interest, or worry about him, or begin to avoid. "It's not about me," he says.

But this reluctance makes it more difficult for his wife, who needs support, and needs to talk about her stepdaughter's illness, but feels she should not because he would not approve.

So, this is mental illness. Or is it? The man's daughter says it is not; in fact, it is a higher form of mental health. She has less anxiety, more peace of mind.

This situation, whatever it is, is tearing the man's family apart. Some family members insist the woman is mentally ill; others think she is spiritually elite. Some cope by avoiding the whole issue, rightfully recognizing they can do nothing. Others cannot stop worrying, obsessing. There have been arguments (one with his ex-wife, the adult child's mother), and will probably be more. It is unsolvable, intractable, immutable. And, it is ever-present.

But is it really a problem? Although the man's daughter was briefly in the hospital, and was released with a prescription (which she immediately began taking less of), she does not appear to be in any danger to herself or anyone else, a necessary criteria for rehospitalization or enforced treatment. She appears to be functioning well in her job and in the community. Only in the home can her peculiarities be seen. There she is quite different: challenging, demanding, disregarding.

This man and his wife both feel alone, even though they have each other and, for that matter, are part of more than one caring community. Feeling alone in a crowd is one of the consequences of the ripple effect mental illness can cause in the fabric of a family. Helplessness, of course, is another. Both must be accepted; but perhaps the loneliness can be addressed.

There are, of course, support groups, many established by organizations like the National Alliance on Mental Illness (NAMI) and the Depression and Bi-Polar Support Alliance, as well as any number of hospitals and community groups. There are also peer support groups within the mental health community, as well as within many religious communities. And, of course, we mental health professionals are quick to encourage family members of the mentally ill to avail themselves of counseling or psychotherapy.

But again, there is still stigma. And so too often we remain, alone, in pain, hiding from the comfort that may well be in plain sight.

Saying "I'm Sorry" to Dressie *

In my defense, I was very young at the time – perhaps 14 – and, I suppose, an angry adolescent. But, then, aren't all 14-year-old boys angry? It comes with the testosterone.

As a farm boy growing up on a farm in the Missouri Ozarks, one of my jobs was to move our small dairy herd between their pasture and the barn, about a quarter of a mile, across a road and a railroad track. Since I spent a lot of time with the cows, we developed a relationship of sorts.

The Alpha Cow (who always took the lead when they walked to or from the pasture), was a black and brown milk cow named Flossy. Also in our herd was Flossy's daughter, who we called Dressie. Dressie was the youngest member of the herd, a bit nervous, and usually took her place toward the back of the pack as they moved to and fro.

Somehow, Dressie and I became close. She would come up to me as we stopped for me to open a gate, and I would talk to her while I rubbed her face. There was a kinship of sorts, I suppose: both of us felt *different*. I was an only child who was out of place in the rough-and-tumble world of rural life; Dressie was much younger than the rest of the herd, and owed her place (tolerated, at best, by the other cows) because of her relationship to her mother.

---

*This story first appeared in the July, 2015, edition of the *Tartan Times*, a publication by the residents of Aberdeen Heights, a senior independent living facility in Kirkwood, Missouri.

One afternoon, as the cows gathered at the gate between the pasture and the barn, Dressie nuzzled me. But I was in a foul mood (who knows why? I was 14), and instead of rubbing her face, I poked her on the nose. Not hard, I think, but a cow's nose is sensitive. Surprised, she stepped back, and never again came close to me. I felt terrible, of course, but some sins cannot be fixed.

I tell you this because apologizing, as a way to be forgiven transgression, is in vogue today. Politicians, celebrities, and even sports icons have apologized for acts public and private, in the hopes that their sins might be forgiven, and they might be able to continue to be revered.

But my experiences have taught me that, while forgiveness may be granted, forgetting does not necessarily ensue. And, for that matter, sometimes apologies are not even possible.

After all, how *could* one apologize to a cow?

Rush, Ron, and 15 Minutes of Fame *

I've told this story to two or three Aberdeen residents recently, so I may as well tell everyone, if for no other reason than to prevent rumors. It concerns my "15 minutes of fame," when Rush Limbaugh mentioned me on the air. Superficially, this column may sound political, but – before you get all worked up – it really isn't. Trust me.

The event was truly a good news – bad news situation: I learned about *der Rushter's* comments from son Steve, who was then living in Spartanburg, South Carolina. I appreciated getting the news, but had to ask Steve "what the hell were you doing listening to Rush?" Then again, considering the context, I'm not sure being mentioned by Rush is actually good news. I'll let you decide.

It happened this way. The time was September or October of 2000, which was, like this one, a presidential election year. Bush v. Gore, as I recall. I was sitting in a booth at C. J. Muggs in Webster Groves, eating a chili size (chili over a burger patty, with a fried egg on top, if you must know the details), and reading a book. Sorry, I don't remember the name of the book. Food I remember; books not so much.

---

*This story first appeared in the February, 2016 edition of the *Tartan Times*, a publication by the residents of Aberdeen Heights, a senior independent living facility in Kirkwood, Missouri.

I was, in other words, minding my own business, when I was interrupted by an attractive young woman, who slid into the seat opposite me and asked if we could talk. She was, she said, from the Associated Press, and was doing a story about people's thoughts about the election. What did I think?

It was late in the campaign year, and I was pretty fed up with the whole thing. (And that was 16 years ago, when politicians were still being civil!) I said, "It seems to me as if they are trying to sell candidates like soap." She smiled, scribbled something on her paper and, sadly, moved on.

Apparently, she included my comment in her article; and apparently Limbaugh read it. According to my son, Rush said, "If Ron Scott of Webster Groves, Missouri, wants to know how to vote, he should just listen to me for five minutes."

That's about right, I thought.

Steve said he was "flipping through the dial" on the car radio when he heard my name and realized it was Rush. Yeah, right. That's his story, and he's still sticking to it.

Steve's Blog: Bettereveryday *

S teve began his blog after he was transferred to the rehabilitation hospital. The blog reflected his dogged determination to make some kind of lemonade out of the very bitter lemons he found when he awoke paralyzed after back surgery.

A few months ago, Steve had begun to experience numbness and weakness in his legs. Within weeks the symptoms were so bad he consulted with a neurosurgeon. Within two months he was scheduled for surgery – risky but essential surgery to repair a herniated thoracic disk. By the date of the surgery Steve could barely walk a few steps; he was clearly headed for the wheelchair he needed to enter the hospital.

Steve and his wife Michele had come home to St. Louis only a few months earlier when Steve, after working across the country as a television news director for more than 20 years, had been hired at KSDK, the TV station his parents had watched the most as he was growing up.

Steve started his blog – what you and I might call a journal – on "tumblr", an internet site designed for such purposes. His blog was intended to serve several purposes: as a way for him to record his recovery, in whatever form that might take place; as a way to keep family and friends informed about what was happening; and as a way to reflect on the changes that were being forced on his and Michele's life.

---

*This story first appeared in the August-September, 2015, edition of the Newsletter of the St. Louis Psychological Association

Psychologists often encourage clients traversing difficult situations to keep a journal. Journals are good ways to process loss, grief, and other life-changing events. However, where journals have, in the past, often been private, blogs, published on the internet, are public. Steve, as a product of his time, is comfortable making public what you and I may have needed to keep private. Times change.

Journaling can, of course, be a path inward, where self-reflection can lead to insight and growth. Steve began his blog by writing:

> I have what they are referring to as an incomplete spinal cord injury. . . . The result of that damage is that I am currently paralyzed from the waist down. This is my story of recovery. . . . I hope to be able to understand my injury, recover from it, or learn the skills to live with what functions I have left. I have chosen to remain positive and share my story along this path of being bettereveryday.

On day 34 he wrote:

> Today [at] shift change. . . . the day nurse. . . . told the new nurse that I was paraplegic. While I know this to be true it is actually the first time I have heard somebody use it in reference to me. . . . The doctors still haven't used the word paraplegic yet because early on it was too early and that is not what they are about here at the rehab hospital and that surely isn't me is it?

And he concluded:

> I am a paraplegic but even if that is permanent I don't want it to define me. I am determined to not make that me. I will still be the same person I am just differently physically. . . . I had 47

years of one life now I have a different one. I have the . . . will
to make everything bettereveryday.

I would like to tell you that Steve began his blog on the advice of
his psychologist step-father, but Steve began his blog on his own, an
awareness that processing painful new truths could make them more
digestible.

It is rewarding to hear such wisdom written by one's child – even
one's 48-year-old child.

All of this has been, as you can imagine, emotionally very painful
for Marilyn and me. Helpless hand-wringing is difficult enough
in any circumstance; when the patient is one of your children, it is
beyond description. And the uncertainty of recovery – what kind
and how much, if any – means that closure (whatever that would
mean) is always somewhere in the future.

Having said that, I must repeat that Steve is determined to
achieve whatever independence is possible. He can, he insists, put
out the news from a wheelchair. Thus, he insists, #bettereveryday is
his mantra.

Made in the USA
Monee, IL
02 April 2022

93983020R00094